HEAR GOD'S VOICE

HEAR
GOD'S
VOICE

Learn to Use the Prophetic
Gift of the Holy Spirit

Dr. Bill Hamon

Christian
International

Content

1

Restoration & Activation of the Gifts of the Spirit

God has restored the five-fold ministry and all nine gifts of the Spirit to the Church today so that She can prepare the way of the Lord and make ready the people for His return. Since we are being established in present truth, we must look at our historic understanding of the gifts of the Spirit with fresh eyes to see what God means by and intends for these gifts today.

In Matthew 16 Jesus says He will build a Church. The Greek word, ekklesia, is used throughout the New Testament when talking about the church. In Greek culture, ekklesia was known as a meeting or gathering of people, often as a ruling body meeting to make decisions and govern a region. The Church, or Ekklesia, is made up of individual believers who are "called out" of the world of darkness to establish the Kingdom of God. Jesus addressed the Church before His ascension, promising power to fulfill Kingdom responsibilities. This power is for every believer: church leaders, business people, parents, teachers, politicians, medical personnel, tradesmen, artists, etc. All believers have the responsibility and the power to influence their world and build the Kingdom of God.

FIVE-FOLD MINISTRY

Jesus Christ established the five-fold ministry to equip the saints for the work of the ministry. Ephesians 4:11-16 states that Jesus has set five "headship" gifts in the Body to perfect or equip each individual member in his/her membership ministry. The "headship" gifts are apostle, prophet, evangelist, pastor, and teacher. Each has been commissioned by the Lord to develop, mature and enable God's saints to find their particular gifts and train them in those particular areas of service.

In addition, 1 Corinthians 12:14-31 reveals that God has set the members in His Body as it has pleased Him and that we "are members in particular." From the beginning, the Lord desired that every member of the Body of Christ be equipped and functioning in their particular area using their natural and supernatural gifts by the grace of God.

SUPERNATURAL GIFTS

The supernatural gifts of the Holy Spirit are an integral part of the equipment that every saint should manifest. 1 Corinthians 12:7 states, "But the manifestation of the Spirit is given to each one for the profit of all." We can learn four lessons from this verse. First, the word "manifestation" is a Greek word that means demonstrate or show. The nine gifts show God's love. Second, they are given, which means they cannot be earned, worked for, bought or achieved. Third, they are given to every believer, which means no one in the body of Christ is to be excluded from experiencing these nine supernatural gifts. Finally, they are given for the profit of all, which means each of us do our part to contribute to the wellbeing of the Body of Christ.

The next three verses (8-10) list the nine gifts that are standard equipment for saints who have received the gift of the Holy Spirit. In verse 11, we are instructed that these gifts are manifested by the same Holy Spirit who divides to every man several of the supernatural gifts as He wills. Every one of the gifts of the Spirit have value. Each is needed at different times in different situations. They are provided so believers can demonstrate God to the world around them.

Jesus put the gifts in His will and when He died and rose again, His will was read in heaven and written by men. God's will is no longer hidden in Jesus or the Holy Spirit, but is openly declared and revealed in a book on Earth: the New Testament of the Bible. Individuals do not need to question aspects of His will if they are revealed as His will in the Bible.

Jesus willed the gifts of the Spirit to the Body of Christ, but the Holy Spirit still divides and distributes those gifts as He desires. All that is written in the New Testament is the inheritance of the saints. Known as God's children, Holy Spirit-baptized saints are all born again, and have been given gifts of the Holy Spirit. Some saints manifest divine abilities more than others, but believers only need to be concerned with what portion of that will is for them to individually receive and manifest. The Lord would not have given us these gifts unless He desired for us to have a working knowledge of them and to use them (1 Corinthians 12:1).

Holy Spirit gifts are one way the Spirit of God reveals Himself to the world through the believer. Two other significant ways in which believers show the character and nature of God to the world are love and the fruit of the spirit. In 1 Corinthians chapters 12 and 14 Paul explains and encourages believers to know and use the Gifts of the Spirit. Chapter 13, right in between these two important chapters, holds the greatest truth that all of the gifts are nothing without love. The fruit of the Holy Spirit in the life of

a believer is also a demonstration of God to the world
(Galatians 5:22-26).

THE TIME HAS COME FOR "ALL THINGS TO BE DONE"

1 Corinthians 14:40 says, "Let all things be done decently and in order." We have concentrated on the
"decently and in order" portion of the Scripture for so
long that most of the Church has overlooked "Let all
things be done." Fearing spiritual "wildfires," they have
quenched the fire! We must allow *all* of God's gifts
(and headship ministry) to function and flow as Jesus
commanded in Scripture.

Psalm 68:1 begins, "Let God arise..." Let us allow
God to arise through us as we yield to Him and His
supernatural gifts. Jesus is ever interceding that His
Church arise as a corporate body, continually maturing and manifesting that which "every joint supplies,
according to the effective working by which every part
does its share..." (Ephesians 4:16).

We must purpose to activate and train God's servants, just as a natural army purposely trains its troops
in warfare techniques before releasing them into battle.
God's leaders must allow time and a place for the saints
to be taught and activated into the gifts and functions
the Lord has placed within them.

FAITH IS ALWAYS THE ACTIVATING FORCE FOR REVELATION

It is faith that activates the gifts—not feelings, signs, sensations, or being spiritually mysterious or bizarre.

Romans 12:6 says, "Having then gifts differing according to the grace that is given to us, let us use them: if prophecy, let us prophesy in proportion to our faith." Our gifts are different according to the grace given us. Grace can be defined as: God's divine unmerited enablement. In other words, God gives us His ability as a gift even though we do not merit it. It is not something we earn or work for, it is a gift given and appropriated by *faith*.

We do not have to feel anything! We do not have to receive "Holy Spirit goose bumps" or stimulate our flesh in order to be used in the Spirit in His gifts. It takes truth, faith and grace to activate and move in the gifts of the Spirit, just as it does to receive Jesus Christ as our Savior.

DIVINE UNMERITED ENABLING AND ACTIVATION

Through divine, unmerited enabling, the saints are challenged with truth to receive the grace to do what the Bible says they can do. Evangelicals, established 400 years ago, have long recognized their privilege to activate the gift of eternal life using Romans 10:9, that if you confess with your mouth the Lord Jesus and believe in your heart that God has raised Him from the dead, you will be saved. Charismatics, established 100 years ago, recognize their responsibility and right to activate the gift of the Holy Spirit in a born again believer.

The prophets and apostles today recognize their ability to activate the saints in the gifts of the Holy Spirit and their responsibility to establish, function and bring order in the "house." Believers are activated in the same manner as the gift of eternal life or the gift of the Holy Spirit.

Activation always follows the same sequence as salvation (Romans 10:9):

- Hearing the Word of Truth (someone ministers truth from the Word of God);
- Believing in the heart (the Holy Spirit overshadows that instruction and illuminates belief in the heart and mind of the hearer);
- Confessing with the mouth (God's grace gives that person the divine unmerited ability to respond); and
- Doing and responding to God by manifesting that grace, not only by hearing, but through faith arising in their heart.

Most Charismatics and Pentecostals agree that they have the right to expect, and the prerogative to activate, the gift of eternal life and/or the gift of the Holy Spirit with evidence of speaking in tongues. Likewise, in both the modern Prophetic/Apostolic and Saints Movements, we have the right to expect, and the prerogative to activate, the individual members in the Body of Christ in the particular gifts of the Spirit that have been imparted to them (Romans 1:11).

Why is it strange when someone says they are going to activate the gifts of the Holy Spirit? Is it because it was unfamiliar in times past, but now it is God's timetable for revelation of 1 Corinthians 12:7-10, for appropriation in the Prophetic/Apostolic and Saints Movements and beyond? The truth of the gift of eternal life by grace and faith is familiar because it was established 400 years ago. The truth of the gift of the Holy Spirit by grace and faith is familiar because it was established over 100 years ago. The truth of the gifts of the Spirit being activated in every believer by grace and faith is far more recent, but just as relevant and vital.

THE RESPONSIBLE GENERATION

We are the generation responsible for establishing every saint in his/her membership ministry. This responsibility includes developing the saints in the gifts of the Spirit because we have been given this mandate and open revelation.

Martin Luther and the reformers of the 1500s were accountable before God to bring an open revelation of the gift of eternal life. (Where would we be today if they had not "run their race"?) The Pentecostal brethren of the early 1900s and the Charismatic brethren of the 1960s were accountable to bring forth the revelations they received.

Today, we are similarly held responsible before God to establish every believer in the present truth of the gifts of the Holy Spirit by teaching, training, and activation, as well as through the validity of five-fold ministers. (Where will the next generation be if we do not?)

> *"Therefore He says: 'Awake, you who sleep, arise from the dead, and Christ will give you light. See then that you walk circumspectly, not as fools but as wise, redeeming the time, because the days are evil. Therefore do not be unwise, but understand what the will of the Lord is. And do not be drunk with wine, in which is dissipation; but be filled with the Spirit.'" (Ephesians 5:14-18)*

Let us take the challenge and venture to the place of moving with God in His current-day timetable.

2

God Wants to Communicate

"But solid food belongs to those who are of full age, that is, those who by reason of use have their senses exercised to discern both good and evil." Hebrews 5:14

God is personal. He desires to communicate. In this chapter, we will talk about His thoughts and personal nature, his desire for intimacy, how sin affected our communication, and what to expect in a personal and intimate relationship with God.

WHY GOD WANTS TO COMMUNICATE

God wants to communicate with us primarily because He is thinking about us:

"How precious also are Your thoughts to me, O God! How great is the sum of them! If I should count them, they would be more in number than the sand; when I awake, I am still with You."
(Psalm 139:17-18)

David describes God's thoughts toward himself—one man—as more than the sands of the seas. Based on this innumerable quantity, God is always thinking about us.

In the 1980s, God spoke to me to move Christian International's headquarters to Florida. We relocated to the panhandle along the Emerald Coast. Today it is a major tourist destination, with over 4,000,000 visitors per year—back then, it was the middle of nowhere with little more than a beach as its attraction.

Ever since I moved to the beach, I have been amazed by how much sand spreads. If even a little patch of sand gets on your clothes after a day at the beach, you could be vacuuming sand out of your car and house for days afterwards. Consider your experiences with sand. Even just a little bit seems innumerable. David chose to describe God's thoughts as "more than the sands of the seas" because His thoughts toward any one of us are so numerous that we could never measure them all—it could take an eternity to even hear them all.

The second reason He wants to communicate with us is that His thoughts have a specific purpose and plan: "for I know the thoughts I have for you […] to give you a hope and a future" (Jeremiah 29:11). He is not thinking about us for His sake only. Imagine if you couldn't stop thinking about the good things in store for a person; you would want to share your thoughts with them too.

The third reason God wants to communicate is that He is relational. God is love (1 John 4:8) and is, therefore, motivated by love. Love motivates one to communicate because love is relational. Relationship is impossible without communication. God even describes Himself as the Living Word. He speaks:

> *For He is our God, and we are the people of His pasture, and the sheep of His hand. Today, if you will hear His voice: Do not harden your hearts, as in the rebellion, as in the day of trial in the wilderness. (Psalm 95:7–8)*

IT IS COMMON FOR GOD TO COMMUNICATE

Biblical history demonstrates God communicating to man and all creation, speaking to the young and old, to sinner and to the saint. In Genesis alone, God spoke over fifty times using the spoken word, visions and dreams. He spoke the earth into existence.[1] He spoke to Adam and Eve.[2] He spoke to the serpent.[3] He spoke to Cain.[4] He spoke to Enoch.[5] He spoke to Noah.[6] He spoke to Abraham.[7] He spoke to Hagar.[8] He spoke to Isaac and Rebekah.[9] He spoke to Jacob.[10] He spoke to Laban.[11] He spoke to Joseph.[12] He spoke to Israel.[13] He even spoke to Pharaoh,[14] the enemy of His people.

God did not stop speaking after Genesis. He spoke to Moses, Joshua, Samuel, David, Solomon, Job, Elijah, Joseph, Pilate's wife, Peter, Paul, John, and even Balaam, a false prophet. If God spoke to these people, why would He treat you and me any differently? Hearing His voice is not unusual; it actually puts us right in good company with many others throughout history!

BENEFITS TO HEARING HIS VOICE

Communication with God is multifaceted and multi-purposed. Hearing His voice not only benefits us personally, but it also benefits the Body of Christ and His Kingdom. The following section details the impacts of hearing His voice.

INTIMACY WITH HIM

The first, and perhaps most prevalent, benefit to hearing Him is that it brings us closer to Him. Intimacy with

God through hearing His voice is key for the Prophetic/Apostolic and Saints Movements. Do you ever think about why God gave us language? The first obvious answer is to communicate with each other. However, even in nature, animals have the ability to communicate in a variety of non-verbal ways. Is it possible that God gave humans language to enable us to communicate with Him? This ability to communicate with Him changes our relationship with Him. Jesus said:

> *"No longer do I call you servants, for a servant*
> *does not know what his master is doing; but I*
> *have called you friends, for all things that I heard*
> *from My Father I have made known to you."*
> *(John 15:15)*

Those who are intimate with each other share their hearts and minds. We are called to know Him at that intimate level. Intimate friends share ideas, thoughts and feelings—so must we with Him. We are to enjoin and enjoy Him through a deeper level of communication. Our examples are Adam and Eve in Genesis 2, Enoch in Genesis 4, Noah in Genesis 6, Abraham in Genesis 12 and 18, and through Jesus Christ, His Son. Intimacy through communication has always been God's intent.

PEACE IN OUR HEARTS

The second benefit to hearing God's voice is that it brings peace to our hearts. His voice comforts and encourages us during trials and adversity (Psalm 23). He gives us wisdom to walk through transition. During discouragement and distress, the voice of the Lord penetrates the heart and causes courage to arise and move forward with direction. Those who listen prosper.

When I was first building our extension colleges, Evelyn and I invested everything we had into developing the ministry with a partner, only to have the entire endeavor fall apart when that partner left us. I had been on the road trying to build the college while my partner ran the administration. When he moved on, we were left with no money, no building, no administration and no business partner. We lost everything. I didn't even have enough gas money to get to the next church. Meanwhile, several prophets came into town and prophesied to me. They said: "I see you ministering around the world. I see nations and platforms of thousands of people. You're a prophet to the nations."

At that time in my life, I had never flown on a commercial airline, and I couldn't imagine flying to another country to minister or to build an extension college when I couldn't even take a Greyhound to my next meeting because I was broke. I said to Evelyn, "Doesn't God know what I'm going through right now? He keeps talking to me about the future, but I need help today!" Always the voice of reason, Evelyn replied, "Bill, don't you think if you're going to do all that in the future that you will make it through today?" That's what God's voice does for us—it comforts us about today by letting us know His heart and intent for our lives from this day forward.

Unity and Purpose to Our Corporate Existence

God sees us as more than individuals. He looks at the corporate Body of Christ worldwide as well as the corporate body in any group gathered for any purpose. When we gather together as a group of believers, God has destiny and purpose planned for our group. By each of us hearing His heart, we come to understand why God brought us together. We discover His divine purpose and destiny for our body of believers. This promotes unity in the Body of Christ as we begin to see ourselves and others fitting together:

> *"the whole body, joined and knit together by what every joint supplies, according to the effective working by which every part does its share, causes growth of the body for the edifying of itself in love." (Ephesians 4:16)*

Until the "house" is complete and ready for habitation, we are in transition with instructive visitations. Jesus declared, "I will build My church" (Matthew 16:18, Ephesians 2:22). The Church is not millions of individuals, though it may be made up of individuals. It is a single unit. When we hear His voice, we can come into greater unity and maturity toward perfection.

Revelation of His Plans for Us

Jeremiah 29:11 says, "I know the plans I have for you […] to give you a hope and a future." God is filled with plans for our lives. He knows what they are—do we? When we hear His voice, we receive strategies and direction for our individual lives, so that we may satisfy our purposes and find fulfillment.

God speaks vision so we can move forward. He speaks wisdom so we know how to conduct our lives. He speaks strategy so we can advance and overcome. He speaks eternal purpose so we have perspective in our circumstances. God's voice is not about predicting our future but rather about decreeing His purpose, so we can align with it and fulfill all He has called us to.

Protection for Our Lives and Interests

God is our fortress, strong-tower, defender and shelter. He will lead us through difficulty into safety.

"He shall call upon Me, and I will answer him;
I will be with him in trouble; I will deliver him
and honor him." (Psalm 91:15)

God sent an angel to Joseph and Mary to warn them of harm intended against their newborn. He spoke to Israel's armies about when to go into battle and let them know He would fight for and defend them. He spoke to King Abimelek and protected him from ignorantly taking Abraham's wife Sarah. He spoke to Israel and informed them that angels had gone ahead to protect them as they took possession of their promised land. He even used a donkey to speak and warn Balaam of danger. Scripture is full of God speaking to people in various ways as a means to protect them from danger.

PROVISION FOR OUR CALLING

One of Jesus' earliest interactions with His disciples was a statement that caused them to have abundance:

And He said to them, "Cast the net on the right
side of the boat, and you will find some." So they
cast, and now they were not able to draw it in
because of the multitude of fish. (John 21:6)

The voice of God will bring prosperity when we hear and obey him.

Transformation

Communication brings reformation from the inside out. As we hear His voice and respond, it matures us and causes us to grow into Him. We are conformed into the image of Jesus: "For whom He foreknew, He also predestined to be conformed to the image of His Son, that He might be the firstborn among many brethren" (Romans 8:29).

God the Father made communication an essential part of our personal transformation process. By discerning His voice, His love and His desires that come alive within our hearts, we long to be like Him and do as He did.

METHODS OF COMMUNICATION

God's desire and design is to have free-flowing communication with mankind. Ever since sin dulled man's ability to hear God's voice, He has chosen other means of communication.

Old Testament Prophets—God's Communication Channels

God initially set up prophets in the Old Testament as his communication channels. At that time, there was no redemption from sin. Jesus had not come yet, so mankind no longer had direct access to God like they did in the Garden of Eden. Since God seeks to communicate, He designated messengers who would speak His message to the people. God called these messengers, or prophets, "My servants" (Jeremiah 35:15). Prophets only spoke in part and understood in part. Sometimes it was direct and clear, while other times they spoke in allegories. Generally, the people disliked the words spoken by prophets and would not listen—some would even abuse or kill them.

Jesus—God's Ultimate Revealer

God then sent His Son, who was more than a prophet, as the verbal and visual manifestation of God's own thoughts, words, principles, and pattern of living. Jesus was the newest and richest point of access to God after the Old Testament prophets. Jesus' arrival on the scene, as well as His death and resurrection, forever changed mankind's ability to access God and showed Him in living form. The Old Testament prophets gave us His Word, but His Son was so much more. The people were able to see His nature in a relatable way—His Words became flesh and dwelt among us.

Jesus fully understood His heavenly Father and expressed Him by speaking and demonstrating the whole counsel of God. Jesus Christ is the brightest display of God's glory and the greatest expression of

God's person ever to occur in eternity. Jesus' redemptive act tore the veil that kept us from viewing God and coming into His presence. He removed the cause of our dullness in hearing God. He is the personification of God dwelling within each believer. Those born again become the temple of God, the dwelling place of the Most High:

> *"Or do you not know that your body is the temple of the Holy Spirit who is in you, whom you have from God, and you are not your own? 20 For you were bought at a price; therefore glorify God in your body and in your spirit, which are God's." (1 Corinthians 6:19)*

Still, some people did not like what Jesus had to say as God's living voice. They crucified Him and killed Him (Acts 3:15, Zech. 12:10). God knew they would. This demonstrates just how much God loves us and wants to communicate with us.

The Bible and History—God in Written Form

God sent a book to enable man to hear the mind, the will and the purposes of God. Scripture is the complete written revelation of God and is all the sacred writing the mortal Church will ever require to carry out the whole will of God. It contains all the knowledge and power of godliness that mankind will need now and through all eternity.

Satan has sought to oppress the Word of God throughout history. He has lied about, stolen and "religionized" the Word of God in order to nullify its power to save. Many men have conspired in this effort and sold out the power of God (His Kingdom) to have their own. The results of their efforts range from discrepancies in interpretation between Christians (as seen in the multitude of denominations) to the misappropriation of entire passages by those who do not believe in Him.

As modern Christians we must remember that the Bible is alive! It is sharper than anything else, able to divide between soul and spirit, and it is life to those who find it and health to all their flesh (Hebrews 4:12-1, Proverbs 4:22).

The Holy Spirit—God's Voice, Teacher and Agent of Truth

When Jesus arose from the dead, He provided the promise of the Holy Spirit. The Holy Spirit is God's agent, with and within us, who leads us into "all truth." The Holy Spirit is the One who gives us the ability to "rightly divide the Word" of God so we can properly understand and apply Scripture.

God speaks his direction to individuals directly through the amplifying and clarifying voice of the Holy Spirit. The Holy Spirit can speak directly to the heart of a person in a number of ways. In the Old Testament, the Holy Spirit came upon the people. In the New Covenant, He is with us and within us. In the quickening pace of God's Restoration Moves, it is imperative to hear the Holy Spirit over doctrinal differences keeping pliable, fresh and new wineskins. As we migrate to the new from glory to glory, we must welcome the "upgrades." There is always more that God is doing! He is a "now" God.

THE PROPHET—GOD'S SPOKESPERSON

God brings revelation or rhema through the Word of God. He even uses others to speak through the voice of prophecy. Prophets are given to the New Testament Church in the wisdom of God. They form a part of the mantle of Jesus which He left behind when He ascended into heaven. Their purpose is to mature the body of Christ and enable them to hear God.

Prophets are those special voices who bring illumination about that which is already written—without additions or subtractions. They are the men and women called and trained to recognize God's voice and express His thoughts and commands for how to edify the body and build the Church. A prophet's ministry is diverse in function and plentiful in purpose. You can read more about the function of prophets in my book *Prophets and Personal Prophecy*.

PROPHECY—THE VOICE OF THE HOLY SPIRIT

In addition to the Holy Spirit and the Holy Scriptures, prophecy is a gift of the Holy Spirit, given to believers to use in the work of the ministry. He has established prophecy as a valid means of bringing forth revelation and illumination, which reveal the mind of Christ to humanity: "I will pour out of My Spirit on all flesh; Your sons and your daughters shall prophesy." (Acts 2:17)

There is always a need for the prophetic voice of the Lord. Paul told the Corinthian Church to "covet to prophesy" (1 Cor. 14:39-40). God wants His will to be vocalized so He uses the ministry of prophecy to give and confirm specific instruction to individuals concerning His will for their lives. It is for edification, exhortation and comfort.

Personal prophecy must never become a substitute for an individual's responsibility and privilege to hear God's voice for themselves. It is a Christian's duty to fast, pray and seek God to hear from heaven. It is also important to note that prophecy should never contradict the Bible. God wants intimacy on a personal level and through personal communication. He is a jealous God (Exodus 20:5).

ANGELS—THE MESSENGERS OF GOD

God still uses angels, seen and unseen, to communicate with us. They speak the words of the Father and do His bidding:

> *But to which of the angels has He ever said: Sit at My right hand, till I make Your enemies Your footstool? Are they not all ministering spirits sent forth to minister for those who will inherit salvation? (Hebrews 1:13-14)*

Additional examples of angelic activity can be found throughout the bible, such as when an angel of the Lord spoke to Philip (Acts 8:26) or in Acts 1:80 when the Holy Spirit guided the apostles as they established the church in Jerusalem. Psalm 103:20 says, "Bless the Lord, you His angels, who excel in strength, who do His word, heeding the voice of His word."

GOD CREATED US TO HEAR HIS VOICE

Hearing God's voice should be easy and frequent. God made our ears to hear! Our ability to hear God is not based on our righteousness—but the effects of sin (such as guilt, hardness of heart, bitterness, unforgiveness, condemnation) can hinder us from opening our spiritual ears to hear His voice.

> *"The hearing ear and the seeing eye, the Lord has made them both." (Proverbs 20:12).*

It is clear by His efforts and provision that God wants to communicate. Adam and Eve fell from grace and still heard God's voice, as did Cain (Genesis 3:8; 4:9-10). God was eager to speak to rebellious Israel. He sought to speak through His prophets, as Jeremiah, even when the children of Israel had no desire to hear His voice and would later kill the very ones God sent to save them.

3

Discerning the Voice of God

> *"This charge I commit to you, son Timothy, according to the prophecies previously made concerning you, that by them you may wage the good warfare."*
> *1 Timothy 1:18*

As we endeavor to gain knowledge about God's voice, one of the key aptitudes to learn is the ability to discern whose voice are we really hearing. As we come understand that God communicates through a variety of different methods, we will also grow to understand that communication on the spirit level is normal to those who are born of the Spirit. This knowledge creates a greater discernment and sensitivity to His voice while releasing within us the ability to cooperate in His will. This cooperation manifests in all gifts:

*For to one is given the word of wisdom through
the Spirit, to another the word of knowledge
through the same Spirit, to another faith by the
same Spirit, to another gifts of healings by the
same Spirit, to another the working of miracles, to
another prophecy, to another discerning of spirits,
to another different kinds of tongues, to another
the interpretation of tongues. (1 Cor. 12:8-10)*

LEARNING TO DISCERN GOD'S VOICE

Discerning God's voice comes from a process of growth. A key to discerning the voice of God is to continually exercise our spiritual ears to hear. "But solid food belongs to those who are of full age, that is, those who by reason of use have their senses exercised to discern both good and evil" (Hebrews 5:14).

Exercise causes us to grow in our ability to differentiate between our human spirit and the voice of the Holy Spirit. His voice is heard with greater clarity and distinction as we spend time with the Father and extend our faith to hear Him. Jesus said, "My sheep hear my voice" (John 10:27). Even though we all have the capacity to hear, we must learn to turn on, tune in and control the volume. Therefore, we not only learn the principles, but also train and bring theory into personal reality, remembering that the flesh resists and hates moving in the Spirit.

A major element of learning to discern God's voice is to acknowledge that we are doing just that—learning. We can accomplish this through humility and in giving ourselves grace. The Scriptures tell us not to despise small beginnings (Zech. 4:10). The slightest ability or growth in hearing God is valuable, but no one has arrived at the end of the learning process. The gifting will continue to grow with use like any muscle and the more we exercise, the more room we will have to learn to discern His voice. So commit to sticking with it until you have taken ownership of the gift—you will begin to steward well what He has given you.

God Speaks Differently to Every Person

A distressing vision is declared to me: Therefore, my loins are filled with pain; Pangs have taken hold of me, like the pangs of a woman in labor. I was distressed when I heard it; I was dismayed when I saw it. (Isaiah 21:2-3)

Here we see three methods in which God communicated to Isaiah: seeing, feeling and hearing. Some say God speaks through mental images or pictures. Others sense physical sensations and heartfelt impressions. Some hear words, or words in thought form. In the Bible, people heard God in a variety of ways:

- Paul heard a voice on the day of his conversion (Acts 9:4);
- Both Cornelius and Peter received instruction from the Lord through visions (Acts 10);
- Joseph had a dream (Genesis 37); and
- Abimelech also had a dream (Genesis 20:3).

God communicates His thoughts and intents in different ways. Remember Balaam and his donkey? This knowledge allows us to appreciate that people hear in different ways. Allow yourself the liberty to discover how you best "hear from heaven" (2 Chronicles 7:14). He may communicate with you in more than one way. Be sensitive and don't limit God. In fact, when we have faith to "hear" from God in more than one way, He is faithful to respond to our faith in Him.

Learn to Discern

Every Christian discovers that God has a primary way in which He speaks to them. Through practice, their ability to discern grows. Finding "there" (where we hear His Voice) within each of us comes by the process of walking by faith. The process is understood by activating, exercising, and measuring. This is similar to the concept of being "caught not taught." Like a police scanner or radio signal, God's voice is constantly transmitting His thoughts and desires. Our spiritual senses can be likened to the different channels on a police radio scanner. Even though God is transmitting on a continual basis, we do not all hear His voice on the same "frequency." Some people are sensitive to dreams, others to an inward witness, and others to hearing a strong Holy Spirit inspired thought or impression. Be sensitive and do not limit God. In time, God may use other ways to speak to you. With use, sensitivity and confidence in hearing His Voice will come.

THREE PRIMARY WAYS GOD COMMUNICATES

By Seeing

Seeing by the Spirit can fall into three categories: mental images, visions and dreams. Mental images are mental pictures received in the human spirit prompted by the Holy Spirit. These are more prevalent than visions or dreams. For example, when the word "apple" is spoken, most people would immediately picture a red, green or yellow apple in their mind's eye. Likewise, the Lord can communicate with our human spirit and bring forth a mental picture. In John 1:48, we see the Father communicating to Jesus about Nathanael in a "picture" for a word of knowledge:

> *Nathanael said to Him, "How do You know*
> *me?" Jesus answered and said to him, "Before*
> *Philip called you, when you were under the fig*
> *tree, I saw you."*

Some people receive instantaneous mental pictures that can be described in great detail. For others, the images develop like Polaroid film giving more and more detail as the picture emerges. The believer, like the camera, opens the shutter of their heart to the Lord—they ask for a divinely inspired thought, and wait upon Him to bring forth a mental image.

Visions are supernatural occurrences where the Lord opens the natural eyes to see into the spiritual realm. As described in the Old Testament, the prophet Elisha communicated with God through a vision:

> *And Elisha prayed, and said, 'Lord, I pray, open*
> *his eyes that he may see.' Then the Lord opened the*
> *eyes of the young man, and he saw. And behold,*
> *the mountain was full of horses and chariots of fire*
> *all around Elisha. (2 Kings 6:17)*

The prophet Isaiah also saw a vision of God: "In the year that King Uzziah died, I saw the Lord sitting on a throne, high and lifted up, and the train of His robe filled the temple." (Isaiah 6:1)

Dreams are like mental pictures or visions, originated by the Holy Spirit, that the Lord chooses to give while a person is asleep. This pictorial form of communication often involves symbols and may include elements that shadow earthly realities. Books like *Dreams and Visions* detail principles of dream interpretation. In Genesis 20:3, "God came to the king Abimelech in a dream by night, and said to him, 'Indeed you are a dead man because of the woman whom you have taken, for she is a man's wife." When Aaron and Miriam were summoned to stand before the Lord later in the Old Testament He said, "Hear now My words: If there is a prophet among you, I, the Lord, make Myself known to him in a vision; I speak to him in a dream" (Numbers 12:6). A further example of the Lord's presence in dreams occurred when "at Gibeon the Lord appeared to Solomon in a dream by night; and God said, 'Ask! What shall I give you?'" (1 Kings 3:5).

By Hearing

Hearing the Lord can come as an audible voice to the ear. More often, however, it comes as a strong mental thought that originates from the Holy Spirit and imbues our human spirit. Proverbs 20:12 states, "The hearing ear and the seeing eye, the Lord has made them both." His Voice can come as a slight impression that does not dominate, and which you may quickly dismiss. But oftentimes, it is the still small voice of the Spirit that people discern when they say, "I heard the Lord say." Elijah experienced this at Horeb:

> *Then He said, "Go out, and stand on the mountain before the Lord." And behold, the Lord passed by, and a great and strong wind tore into the mountains and broke the rocks in pieces before the Lord, but the Lord was not in the wind; and after the wind an earthquake, but the Lord was not in the earthquake; and after the earthquake a fire, but the Lord was not in the fire; and after the fire a still small voice. So it was, when Elijah heard it, that he wrapped his face in his mantle and went out and stood in the entrance of the cave. Suddenly a voice came to him, and said, "What are you doing here, Elijah?" (1 Kings 19:11)*

Similarly in Isaiah 30:21, the Lord comes as a voice to the sinner saying, "Your ears shall hear a word behind you, saying, 'This is the way, walk in it,' Whenever you turn to the right hand or whenever you turn to the left." It is like a nudging at the back of the mind and may not always be in the prevalent part of our thoughts. God's voice is still and quiet.

In the Bible, there are many instances of the people opening their hearts and minds to hear the Voice of the Lord:

> *And Jeroboam said to his wife, "Please arise, and disguise yourself, that they may not recognize you as the wife of Jeroboam, and go to Shiloh. Indeed, Ahijah the prophet is there, who told me that I would be king over this people" [...] Now the Lord had said to Alijah, "Here is the wife of Jeroboam, coming to ask you something about her son, for he is sick. Thus, and thus you shall say to her; for it will be, when she comes in, that she will pretend to be another woman." (1 Kings 14:2, 5)*

> *For the Lord had caused the army of the Syrians to hear the noise of chariots and the noise of horses — the noise of a great army; so they said to one another, "Look, the king of Israel has hired against us the kings of the Hittites and the kings of the Egyptians to attack us!" (2 Kings 7:6)*

> *Now the Lord came and stood and called as at other times, "Samuel! Samuel!" And Samuel answered, "Speak, for Your servant hears." (1 Samuel 3:10)*

God's voice sounds like your own inner voice. Listening is a skill and you must remain teachable and flexible as you learn to listen for it. Anticipate receiving with an open heart and draw from God—but refrain from going "totally blank." Keep a look out for the thoughts because they often come very fast and are easily overlooked or erased while we are looking for something more complicated. Begin with what you have and let Him expand as you speak out. It can flow as prayer flows from our lips.

By Feeling

Impressions (or sensing) is the unspoken language of the Spirit. This experience is sometimes called a "witness of the Spirit." This experience can mean feeling the emotions of another person—a slight impression in one's spirit, confirmed by a peace of the heart. It can be a deep inward knowing about a situation or person. The Spirit can also be felt through a physical impression, like a word of knowledge about healing that creates a sensation within one's own body. When these sensations arise, it is important to follow peace.

Throughout the Bible, there are numerous examples of the Lord communicating through impressions:

"While he was sitting on the judgment seat, his wife sent to him, saying, 'Have nothing to do with

that just Man, for I have suffered many things
today in a dream because of Him."'
(Matthew 27:19)

"For we do not have a High Priest who cannot
sympathize with our weaknesses, but was in all
points tempted as we are, yet without sin."
(Hebrews 4:15)

"For you had compassion on me in my chains, and
joyfully accepted the plundering of your goods,
knowing that you have a better and an enduring
possession for yourselves in heaven. Therefore, do
not cast away your confidence, which has great
reward." (Hebrews 10:34–35)

In Jesus' ministry, feelings of compassion were evident
many times before He did many signs and wonders:

"But when He saw the multitudes, He was
moved with compassion for them, because they
were weary and scattered, like sheep having no
shepherd." (Matthew 9:36)

"And when Jesus went out, He saw a great
multitude; and He was moved with compassion
for them and healed their sick." (Matthew 14:14)

"And Jesus, when He came out, saw a great multitude and was moved with compassion for them, because they were like sheep not having a shepherd. So, He began to teach them many things."
(Mark 6:34)

"I have compassion on the multitude, because they have now continued with Me three days and have nothing to eat." (Mark 8:2)

"But a certain Samaritan, as he journeyed, came where he was. And when he saw him, he had compassion." (Luke 10:33)

Regardless of how we perceive Him, as we press in to follow the divine thoughts of God, He will lead us to a wellspring of thoughts and wisdom from His heart.

4

Christ's Commands Concerning Spiritual Gifts

"Therefore, I remind you to stir up the gift of God which is in you through the laying on of my hands." 2 Timothy 1:6

Someone once said, "Treasure is only valuable if it's hidden in a place worth looking for." Imagine we were seeking something valuable to possess, but it was out in the open instead of being hidden. Our desire for that treasure would be like a raging fire. The anticipation just to receive or claim it would send us into an emotional frenzy. In situations like that, the thought of happiness and the possibility of our dreams coming true becomes the very vehicle that carries us. We experience the same feeling of anticipation when it comes to the spiritual gifts of God. In this chapter, we will expound on the commands from the Word concerning spiritual gifts; this will work to reveal to the Body of Christ that God wants us to function in the gifts of the Spirit. As we follow the nine commands Christ gives us concerning spiritual gifts, we participate in building the body of Christ together, each doing our part. The Word will show us that the impossible is possible when we believe.

COVET EARNESTLY

To covet means to have tremendous zeal. It is a longing to be used; an intense hunger to see something happen. The Greek word for "covet earnestly" is Zeloo which means to have great desire for, to be jealous over and to be zealously affected. The root word is Zelos which means fervency of mind (hot), or an emotional jealousy (such as a husband would have over his wife). It is a word relating to the positive, sanctified, lust-driving force that will compel the believer to move beyond human reason and selfish pride. It is a compelling force that causes the believer to take a leap of faith into the spiritual realm in order to bless others, regardless of circumstances or the desire to stay within their comfort zone. It is the only spiritual blessing we are told to covet.

There is strong instruction and encouragement to move in the gifts of the Spirit AS we are growing and maturing in Christ. This process works simultaneously. Human reasoning says, "I must be matured first, professional and accomplished, then I can operate in the gifts." But God tells us to covet earnestly the gifts of the Spirit, right now. But why are we supposed to covet using these gifts? Because spiritual gifts are not designed to benefit us directly. They are meant to build up others. 1 Corinthians 14:4 says, "He who speaks in a tongue edifies himself, but he who prophesies edifies the church." Spiritual covetousness takes unselfish, dedicated, humble Christians who are willing to be used in the gifts. We are to manifest the attitude of the heart that says, "I want to be a blessing and a servant to others" (Matthew 23:11; Mark 9:35).

Of the nine gifts of the Holy Spirit, the only gift for our personal edification and comfort is the gift of tongues. The other gifts are for the benefit of others!

"But you, beloved, building yourselves up on your most holy faith, praying in the Holy Spirit." (Jude 1:20)

"For if I pray in a tongue, my spirit prays, but my understanding is unfruitful. What is the conclusion then? I will pray with the spirit, and

*I will also pray with the understanding. I will
sing with the spirit, and I will also sing with the
understanding." (1 Cor. 14:14-15)*

We should covet spiritual gifts because by using them
rightly is an unselfish way, we contribute to the growth
and wellbeing of the people around us. By using the
gifts of the Spirit, we are building the Kingdom of God.

DESIRE SPIRITUAL GIFTS

To reinforce the value God places on us using spiritual gifts, He tells us to desire them. As He yearns for
man's salvation, He is willing to supply the faith and
grace needed for us to use His gifts. He longs for His
Church to expectantly, eagerly and perpetually desire
the gifts that He has given...given...given! To "follow
after love" is the manifest, mature, Christ-like character and the greatest command. It is the measuring stick
of success—for the heart is sewn to Christ.

Desire also comes from the same Greek word
Zeloo and is a key to receiving from God. In 1 Corinthians 14:1, we are told to "pursue love, and desire
spiritual gifts, but especially that you may prophesy."
This concept is also present in Mark 11:24: "Therefore
I say to you, whatever things you ask when you pray,
believe that you receive them, and you will have them."

God wants fruitfulness in our lives. Jesus gives four keys for bringing forth things of the spiritual realm:

- Desire: to crave, desire, or beg (from the Greek word *aiteo*)
- Pray: to communicate or talk with the Lord (from the Greek word *proseuch*)
- Believe: to put one's trust in (from the Greek word *pisteuo*)
- Have: have, come to pass, it will be (from the Greek word *esomai*)

The first step to see a manifestation of God's power, presence or provision is to have an attitude of the heart that craves something godly.

Delight in Hebrew is *anaa*, which means to be soft and pliable. "Delight yourself also in the Lord, and He shall give you the desires of your heart" (Psalm 37:4). Another way to understand desiring is to think of it as becoming like "new wineskin" (Matthew 9:16). David reveals that we are soft and pliable in the hands of God, and the Lord will implant His desires, His cravings and His yearnings into the hearts and minds of believers (Psalm 37). Desire and covet are biblical commands; therefore, full right and authority is given to us to want, expect and *do* the Word.

Ephesians 5:26 tell us "that He might sanctify and cleanse her with the washing of water by the word." As every saint allows God's Word to wash them, each becomes a pliable vessel in His hands, developing an intense desire and craving for the gifts of the Spirit to serve effectually.

The apostolic/prophetic restoration move of God cannot just be bolted onto the existing Church like a room addition—it must restructure the whole onto Scriptural foundations. The apostolic/prophetic pattern is to bring change—to blow away the ashes of all that is false, to raise the dead and obsolete traditions of men that hinder the Church from maturing into the "stature of the fullness of Christ" (Ephesians 4:13).

It is God's restoration move to reestablish and build on the true foundation of Ephesians 2:20.

> *"Having been built on the foundation of the apostles and prophets, Jesus Christ Himself being the chief cornerstone." (Ephesians 2:20)*

The emerging Church, a vital growing entity, must remain soft (sensitive and humble) and pliable (to hear, bow and move swiftly) to the commands of our Lord. He is the Head of the Body.

STIR UP YOUR SPIRITUAL GIFT

We are responsible to stir up the gifts God has given us. Paul's admonition to young Timothy makes this action clear—he must do so by purposeful and premeditated action (activation). The Greek word for "stir up" is *anazopureo*, which means to rekindle or arouse from dormancy. In 1 Timothy 4:14, Paul previously admonished Timothy not to "neglect the gift." The Greek word for "neglect" is *ameieio*, which means to make light of, have no regard for, to be negligent: "Therefore, I remind you to stir up the gift of God which is in you through the laying on of my hands" (2 Timothy 1:6).

Stirring up is done by the individual's own will. Believers do not have to wait on the Holy Spirit unction, but by an act of the human will, we can arouse the gift from a state of dormancy and activate our spiritual prayer/praise language.

"But be doers of the word, and not hearers only, deceiving yourselves." (James 1:22f)

"Thus also faith by itself, if it does not have works, is dead. But someone will say, 'You have faith, and I have works.' Show me your faith without your works, and I will show you my faith by my works. You believe that there is one God. You do well. Even the demons believe—and tremble! But do you want to know, O foolish man, that faith without works is dead?" (James 2:17-20)

> *"For if I pray in a tongue, my spirit prays, but*
> *my understanding is unfruitful. What is the*
> *conclusion then? I will pray with the spirit, and*
> *I will also pray with the understanding. I will*
> *sing with the spirit, and I will also sing with the*
> *understanding." (1 Corinthians 14:14-15)*

The operations of the gifts of God are not based upon feeling but upon the will of the individual to believe the Scriptures and yield to the Spirit of God. It does not require "goose bumps" or "funny feelings." It does not require "being moved by the Spirit" or feeling some manifestation. It requires action. It is written in 1 Timothy 2:4 that it is His will that all men come to saving knowledge of Jesus Christ. Just as salvation is based on our will and His will is established, so it is the Lord's will that every believer rekindle, activate and stir up their spiritual gifts.

How to Stir up the Gifts

The Corinthian Church was carnal, selfish, fleshly, and babes in Christ. The first thing the Apostle Paul did with new Spirit-filled believers was to activate them in the gifts. The Corinth model was to first learn, then put into place operating systems that keep order. As you begin to stir up the gifts of the Holy Spirit, learn, train and activate as you would a young child; give broad parameters, enable movement forward and endeavor into a higher level. Exercise and growth are imperative and are both required to mature. Be convinced it is the Lord's will to manifest His gifts and be persuaded that every believer has at least one of the nine gifts. Realize that no believer is perfect or is expected to be without fault—all will make mistakes.

The second way to activate the gifts of the Lord is to pray in the Spirit; this is both our privilege and a catalyst to receive the mind of Christ. Praying switches on His power source so that our human spirit can receive thoughts, impressions, pictures, and sounds from the Holy Spirit. This is a marvelous guard against the pride of man in his own abilities. We need to go to Him in humble obedience of faith, praying and seeking His wisdom and ways.

Finally, engage your faith. It is not begging, fasting or pleading but a direct gift from God that is to be readily received and poured out. If you know the gift is available to you, you can use it. In 2 Samuel 5, David inquired of the Lord about the Philistines and was given specific instructions by Him—he was commanded to bestir himself. The word "bestir" has three meanings: to be alert, to decide, and to point sharply. You can use your faith like David did, and "be sober" (1 Peter 4:7) and alert to the opportunity. Commit beforehand to taking the opportunity to use the gift—be obedient and trust in our Mighty God. As you engage your faith, "point sharply." In a similar way to being pricked on the finger by something sharp, this focus will awaken and arouse you to full alertness.

David, by his will, obeyed and reaped the benefits—destroying the enemy. Likewise, by obedience, we will reap the benefit of the gifts of the Spirit manifesting.

EXERCISE BY USE

It is by constant use that we develop our spiritual senses. Repeated use teaches us to discern and perceive in the spiritual Kingdom and grow into the full manifestation of gifting. Just as one visit to a gym does not make a man "Mr. Universe," developing spiritual gifts takes continual exercise and directed, dedicated practice. Discernment is developed through use, not just preaching and teaching.

Prophecy is a tool to build and cause migration to a higher level. Foundational prophetic ministry, operating in a high degree, speaks from a future perspective into the present in order to build something valid to advance the Church forward. It speaks into core issues and shakes complacency: "But solid food belongs to those who are of full age, that is, those who by reason of use have their senses exercised to discern both good and evil" (Hebrews 5:14).

Our ability to hear has eternal consequences. Malachi declared that the saints will "again discern between the righteous and the wicked, between one who serves God and one who does not serve Him" (Malachi 3:16-18). Every Spirit-filled believer has gifts that they must exercise. Through this practice they will cultivate spiritual discernment which will be an integral part of ruling and reigning with Christ.[15]

THE PARABLES OF STEWARDSHIP

The parables of stewardship reveal our individual responsibilities to use what we have. Good stewards are accountable once they bear the truth. In Matthew 25:14-30, Jesus shares a parable of stewardship that emphasizes the believer's responsibility to use what the Master imparts. It states that a man traveling into a far country (representing Christ), called his servants (representing the saints) and gave them his goods (symbolic of the Holy Spirit and His gifts). As the parable progresses, we see that the master's servants are given talents according to their abilities. One servant is given five talents, one is given two talents and the last is given one. The first two servants used what they had been given, thereby doubling their talents (v. 16-17). Both received a commendation from their master who stated, "Well done, good and faithful servant; you have been faithful over a few things, I will make you ruler over many things" (v. 23). The servant who hid his talent rather than use it is rebuked by the master who announces, "you wicked and lazy servant." Because of the servant's fear (v. 25), he was reluctant to exercise and use the talents given him.

The parable concludes with the unprofitable servant forfeiting his original talent to the servant who had proven his ability to use (double) his five talents. Matthew 25:29 is impactful with the truth: "For to everyone who has, more will be given, and he will have abundance; but from him who does not have, even what he has will be taken away." The whole counsel of God states in Romans 11:29, "For the gifts and the calling of God are irrevocable."

We are accountable in this life to use what is given to us. God rewards risk done in faith, not reluctance. We must resist the fleshly (self-serving) mind, for the flesh wars with moving in the Spirit. As we faithfully use the gifts God has given each of us, we can expect an increase in ability, wisdom, and grace. However, if we fail to step out in faith, we may be considered wicked and slothful servants of the Lord.

BE NOT IGNORANT

There is danger in being ignorant. In 1 Corinthians, the Holy Spirit emphasizes that He not only wants the saints to hear about the gifts, but desires that they have a workable knowledge that has come from use. Ignorance is defined as lacking or destitute of knowledge, information, comprehension or education; uninformed or unaware; inexperienced or unfamiliar . The last two key words are essential in our understanding, for the Body of Christ has been kept from operating in gifts or have not been given a place to express their gifts; therefore, there is no validation. Hosea 4:6 says, "My people are destroyed for lack of knowledge."

The gifts are unfamiliar because getting to know something comes from experience. The word "ignorant" in Greek is *aanoeo,* which means to ignore, to not know by lack of information, or to not understand or have a workable and experiential knowledge. The prophetic "blows the ashes" off the living foundation of Jesus Christ and His eternal Word. The flame of truth arises, forging new weapons (the Saints moved by the zeal of the Lord) for His eternal plans and purposes. No weapon formed against them shall prosper (Isaiah 54:16).

The apostolic church breaks dead traditions and sets Godly order and government. There is an appreciation of our heritage, but there is also a thrust to keep moving forward. Maturing is a process of progression, not stagnation. Pioneers stay on the cutting edge, and other believers follow the breakthrough upon the swelling wave that follows.

Paul gave his guidelines to educate and direct, not to devalue or quench. The church at Corinth was having difficulties with the gifts of the Spirit. Paul, through the Holy Spirit, brought divine order. To emphasize the Lord's desire for His people to continue manifesting in the gifts, Paul concluded chapter 12 with, "But earnestly desire the best gifts. And yet I show you a more excellent way" (1 Corinthians 12:31).

Considered the "Great Love Chapter," chapter 13 of 1 Corinthians shows that a knowledge of the gifts is not enough—there must be a higher and holy motive of divine love. Paul concludes the guidelines with this powerful statement: "Therefore, brethren, desire earnestly to prophesy, and do not forbid to speak with tongues. Let all things be done decently and in order" (1 Corinthians 14:39-40).

LET ALL THINGS BE DONE DECENTLY AND IN ORDER

Paul admonishes the Corinthians to "covet to prophesy." His guidelines were meant to construct—not to constrict or hinder believers. Paul's guidelines helped the Corinthians overcome their ignorance of the spiritual gifts, just as they were guided through the difficulties they were having with holy communion (1 Corinthians 11).

We have forfeited the Scripture of "let all things be done" and have concentrated more on "decently and in order" (1 Corinthians 14:40). Many of those concerned about "wildfires" have doused all fire. Fearing extremes, we have neglected to encourage a regular manifestation of the gifts that edify, exhort and build up the Body. The apostolic enhances the gifts and gives structure, decency and order. The most difficult part is getting things to be done! So the encouragement to "do" is primary and the building of accuracy is molded while doing it.

GAINING KNOWLEDGE

Gaining knowledge is the beginning of manifesting gifts by faith. Before a believer can manifest anything by faith, he must first come to knowledge of the truth in the Word of God. Romans 10:17 says, "So then faith comes by hearing, and hearing by the word of God." Note that the manifestation of the gift of prophecy is in direct proportion to the faith of the giver! James 2:17 reminds us that faith without corresponding action is dead. We are without excuse! The natural progression is: knowing, believing, receiving and then activating/manifesting by faith. Just as in salvation, so it is in the operations of giftings.

Scripture plainly reveals that God does not want His Church to lack a workable and experiential knowledge of His gifts. The Berean model is revelation, validation, and application!

> *"Having then gifts differing according to the grace that is given to us, let us use them: if prophecy, let us prophesy in proportion to our faith." (Romans 12:6)*

NEGLECT NOT

"Neglect not" is a scriptural command. Christ realized the Church would need the gifts of the Holy Spirit in order to obtain "so great a salvation" (Hebrews 2:3). Regard the gifts of the Holy Spirit as precious and of a most high value:

> *"Do not neglect the gift that is in you, which was given to you by prophecy with the laying on of the hands of the eldership." (1 Timothy 4:14)*

> *"How shall we escape if we neglect so great a salvation, which at the first began to be spoken by the Lord, and was confirmed to us by those who heard Him, God also bearing witness both with signs and wonders, with various miracles, and gifts of the Holy Spirit, according to His own will?" (Hebrews 2:3-4)*

Timothy had a problem not unlike many of us—he had a fear of man. Still, the command rings: neglect not. We are required to "press in." How much do you want the Kingdom in you? We are to run our race and press toward the high mark of our calling.

DESPISE NOT

In 1 Thessalonians 5:19-20, Paul gives a Holy Spirit command: "Do not quench the Spirit. Do not despise prophecies." According to Scripture, there were a number of believers who began to quench the gifts of the Spirit and were growing to despise the spiritual gift of prophecy. The Greek word for "despise" is *exoudenoo*, meaning to make utterly nothing of. The believers did not give the gifts their proper place or order; instead, they gave prophecy a lesser esteem than God commands. He commands us to grant the gifts of the Spirit their proper place and importance in both church and life. We cannot have an attitude of "take it or leave it" and shrug off what He values. Christ commands His Church to "despise not."

BECOME ADDICTED

"I urge you, brethren—you know the household of Stephanas, that it is the first fruits of Achaia, and

*that they have devoted themselves to the ministry
of the saints." (1 Corinthians 16:15)*

This household served in natural ways and also by the gifts of the Holy Spirit. They gained good reputation with Paul as being addicted to serving God's Saints. How better to serve one another than to minister healing in the fellowship, to comfort with prophecy, to bring deliverance with the gift of faith and discerning of spirits, and to show a way with a word of wisdom? The true Church in operation is full of participators, not spectators!

The apostolic pattern is servanthood in spiritual dimensions. Our goal should be to serve the corporate body—to share, encourage with a "now" testimony, and to grow and become servants. We should always be ready to minister to one another and prepared to step out and put ourselves on the line. The Saints craved the opportunity to serve because they knew God's will was to minister.

The Prophetic/Apostolic and Saints Movements bring an anointing to awaken, teach, train and release a new thrust of the Holy Spirit. Preaching is not a Sunday matinee, but a living demonstration of our living God reaching out to meet the needs of His creation. Ministry means having the expectation that every day of the week, the Kingdom will manifest with the "greater works" Jesus proclaimed to His Church, to fulfill all His plan and purposes on Earth. Get addicted!

WE MUST MANIFEST MEMBERSHIP MINISTRY

Every saint has a membership ministry. First Corinthians 12:27 says, "Now you are the body of Christ, and members individually." Paul's concise lecture communicates the necessity that the many members of the Church work together: "But now God has set the members, each one of them, in the body just as He pleased" (v. 18). As a Body of individual members, with gifts differing according to the grace given (Romans 12:6), every believer is commanded to fulfill their individual membership ministry without division, partiality or competition.

We are commanded to minister to one another. First Peter 4:10 says, "As each one has received a gift, minister it to one another, as good stewards of the manifold grace of God."

The New International Version (NIV) states it this way: "Each one should use whatever gift he has received to serve others, faithfully administering God's grace in its various forms." Manifesting the gifts brings edification and growth:

"From whom the whole body, joined and knit together by what every joint supplies, according to the effective working by which every part does its share, causes growth of the body for the edifying of itself in love." (Ephesians 4:16)

As individual members of the Body of Christ manifest their spiritual gifts, they supply the Body's needs, bringing forth a healthy and growing body. Therefore covet, desire, stir up, exercise, be not ignorant, neglect not, despise not, be addicted, and manifest the gifts. Get going!

5

Ministering the Mind of Christ

*"As each one has received a gift, minister
it to one another, as good stewards of the
manifold grace of God." 1 Peter 4:10*

As we explore the wonders of the prophetic ministry, the ability to minister the mind of Christ will always be a components of this amazing gift. This chapter will demonstrate the importance of the human mind and how the spirit works in relation to the supernatural. It will teach and encourage believers how to cultivate their spiritual minds. It will enable them to sharpen their spiritual capacity to hear the Voice of God. Ultimately, it will bring an understanding of the five mind types revealed in Scripture.

THE SPIRITUAL MIND

The spiritual mind is the mind of every born-again, Spirit-filled believer. We are given the mind of Christ according to 1 Corinthians 2:16: "For who has known the mind of the Lord that he may instruct Him? But we have the mind of Christ." We also know it is possible to not utilize our spiritual mind: "For to be carnally minded is death, but to be spiritually minded is life and peace" (Romans 8:6). We have a choice available to us: the spiritual mind we receive when we are made new in Christ, and the carnal mind we were originally born into. Therefore, "let this mind be in you which was also in Christ Jesus" (Philippians 2:5).

Cultivating our spiritual mind is our responsibility—it will not cultivate itself. Every Christian has been given the mind of Christ to steward. This is the mind transformed by renewing by the Word of God. Romans 12:2 exhorts us: "Do not be conformed to this world, but be transformed by the renewing of your mind." The following are six attributes of the spiritual mind:

1. The spiritual mind has thoughts originating from Christ in agreement with the written (logos) Word of God.

2. The spiritual mind functions in divinely inspired thoughts and impressions, not thoughts based upon one's doctrine, attitude, or education.

3. It is in the mind where thoughts originate and are ministered from your redeemed spirit. "Therefore, if anyone is in Christ, he is a new creation; old things have passed away; behold, all things have become new" (2 Corinthians 5:17).

4. The spiritual mind is controlled by the fruit of the Holy Spirit. "But the fruit of the Spirit is love, joy, peace, longsuffering, kindness, goodness, faithfulness, gentleness, self-control. Against such there is no law" (Galatians 5:22-23).

5. This mind's thoughts are in harmony with the letter and Spirit of the Scriptures, a mind in which Kingdom principles prevail. "Finally, brethren, whatever things are true, whatever things are noble, whatever things are just, whatever things are pure, whatever things are lovely, whatever things are of good report, if there is any virtue and if there is anything praiseworthy — meditate on these things" (Philippians 4:8).

6. This is the mind through which the gifts of the Spirit operate. It is motivated and controlled by love (1 Corinthians 13).

It is important to become especially familiar with the spiritual mind and its attributes. When we learn these attributes, we will be able to more quickly recognize when thoughts originate from this mind or from somewhere else.

THE SOULISH MIND

The soulish mind is our natural mind, will, and emotions. God has graced it with such great capacities as memory, creativity, and imagination. It can be thought of as a combination of the natural and spiritual components of thinking. It involves our human capacity to imagine and produce self-motivated ideas to creatively plan and make strategies. This is our God-given capacity, but it does not automatically make the ideas that come from our mind God's ideas. The following characteristics are found in the soulish mind:

- The ability to perceive beyond what evidence or circumstances reveal—a soulish sensitivity, intuition or psychic abilities.
- The realm in which some receive and function in exceptional gifts with special abilities beyond the normal, such as in music, math, and/or memory.
- A mind that tries to control and direct while ministering spiritually.
- A mind that tries to operate on biblical knowledge without a spiritual mind, thereby lacking a personal, intimate relationship with God.
- A mind that tries to manipulate divine things for selfish purposes as with Simon the sorcerer

in Acts 8:9-24. His desire was to have the ability to lay hands on and impart the gift of the Holy Spirit for unholy purposes.

- A mind that uses and manipulates others by using spiritual abilities. This mind understands the gifts, but chooses to control and direct others through disguise of a "prophecy" or "word from the Lord."

THE NATURAL MIND

The natural mind is the most basic aspect of the human mind. "And the Lord God formed man of the dust of the ground and breathed into his nostrils the breath of life; and man became a living being" (Genesis 2:7).

The natural mind is amoral, meaning it produces normal thoughts that are neither good nor bad. A natural mind is trained, skilled, and educated for natural things, such as a doctor or builder who learn skills in their trade. Jesus had a natural mind that enabled him to be a carpenter. The natural mind gives the ability to live and function—to make daily decisions in necessary life processes. It is also a part of the body's anatomy and is the control center of the human body. Through the natural mind we process pain, feel heat and cold, retain memory, laugh, and keep our heart beating and lungs breathing.

THE CARNAL MIND

The carnal mind is the mind of those who have allowed themselves to be consumed with carnal thoughts and desires. According to Romans 8:6-7, the carnal mind is at enmity with God:

> *"For to be carnally minded is death, but to be spiritually minded is life and peace. Because the carnal mind is enmity against God; for it is not subject to the law of God, nor indeed can be."*

In 1 Corinthians, Paul speaks to Christians who have allowed themselves to maintain a carnal mind rather than renewing their minds according to Scripture:

> *"And I, brethren, could not speak to you as to spiritual people but as to carnal, as to babes in Christ. I fed you with milk and not with solid food; for until now you were not able to receive it, and even now you are still not able; for you are still carnal. For where there are envy, strife, and divisions among you, are you not carnal and behaving like mere men? For when one says, 'I am of Paul,' and another, 'I am of Apollos,' are you not carnal?" (1 Corinthians 3:1-4)*

The carnal mind can be made subject to Christ and be renewed. In its carnal state, however, it is exemplified by thoughts that originate from the lust of flesh, the lust of the eyes and the pride of life. These thoughts identify with and promote the works of the flesh:

> *Now the works of the flesh are evident, which are: adultery, fornication, uncleanness, lewdness, idolatry, sorcery, hatred, contentions, jealousies, outbursts of wrath, selfish ambitions, dissensions, heresies, envy, murders, drunkenness, revelries, and the like; of which I tell you beforehand, just as I also told you in time past, that those who practice such things will not inherit the kingdom of God."*
> *(Galatians 5:19-21)*

This is a mind consumed with sensual and evil thoughts. These are thoughts, impressions or feelings that can be demonically inspired.

THE REPROBATE MIND

The reprobate mind is the rarest and most extreme mind a person can operate in. According to Scripture, the reprobate mind is given to those who knowingly refuse truth and allow themselves to be deceived by their evil and self-serving desires.

It is possible God will allow us to be deceived if we willfully refuse the truth:

> *"And with all unrighteous deception among those who perish, because they did not receive the love of the truth, that they might be saved. And for this reason, God will send them strong delusion, that they should believe the lie."*
> *(2 Thessalonians 2:10–11)*

While we cannot know for certain how much willful rejection of truth is enough for us to receive a reprobate mind, we know we can avoid it by keeping our hearts open to receiving the truth and submitting our desires to God. The reprobate mind did not become this way overnight. It is not obtained by mistake but by conscious and continual rejection of God's truth. Its conscience has been seared, perhaps repeatedly: "Speaking lies in hypocrisy, having their own conscience seared with a hot iron" (1 Timothy 4:2). Having forsaken and rejected God, this mind is turned over to self-delusion and demonic obsession:

> *"And even as they did not like to retain God in their knowledge, God gave them over to a debased mind, to do those things which are not fitting."*
> *(Romans 1:28).*

In this turned over state, the mind has become degenerate and depraved. It is deceived, so it defines itself as good but is no longer qualified for good:

> *"They profess to know God, but in works they*
> *deny Him, being abominable, disobedient, and*
> *disqualified for every good work." (Titus 1:16; see*
> *also 2 Timothy 3:8).*

THE MIND IS LIKE THE SOIL OF THE EARTH

Our mind is like soil. We tend to it by planting, watering, and harvesting our thoughts with actions. Sometimes we plant intentionally, but much of what is planted happens unintentionally by way of our surroundings, experiences, relationships and more. While we do not choose all the seeds our mind gets exposed to, we do choose whether we uproot or continue to feed a particular seed as it grows.

Jesus tells the "Parable of the Sower" which describes four minds as four types of ground or soil. This parable is rich with tremendous insight:

> *"Then he told them many things in parables,*
> *saying: "A farmer went out to sow his seed. As he*

was scattering the seed, some fell along the path,
and the birds came and ate it up. Some fell on
rocky places, where it did not have much soil. It
sprang up quickly, because the soil was shallow.
But when the sun came up, the plants were
scorched, and they withered because they had no
root. Other seed fell among thorns, which grew up
and choked the plants. Still other seed fell on good
soil, where it produced a crop—a hundred, sixty or
thirty times what was sown." (Matthew 13:3-8)

FOUR TYPES OF PEOPLE

When we consider the mind as being like soil, we find four distinct types of people:

1. WAYSIDE-SIDEWALK SOIL

Jesus equated this type of person to those who lack the ability to receive or retain truth. They are like cement sidewalks, so hard and barren that the truth of His Word seemingly bounces off. It can also refer to those so open, vulnerable and full of doubt and unbelief that truth never takes root. It is "hardpan" with no loamy soil in which a seed can rest. There is no heart for the truth. 2 Thessalonians 2:10-12 warns this:

*"because they did not receive the love of the truth,
that they might be saved. And for this reason, God
will send them strong delusion, that they should
believe the lie, that they all may be condemned
who did not believe the truth but had pleasure in
unrighteousness."*

2. Shallow-Stony Soil

These people are shallow, and the truth does not take deep root within them because they have no deep-rooted character within themselves. They are selfish people who yield to the pressures of others—this earns them a reputation as people-pleasers, not God-pleasers. Because they are so full of things other than God, there is little fertile soil in which to plant seed.

3. Thorny-Mixture Soil

These people are material-minded and worldly. They have good soil and great potential but have never allowed themselves to be cultivated. Within their hearts lay weed seeds which eventually sprout and choke out any truth that has germinated.

4. Good Ground

These people have allowed God to deeply plow their soil and have learned to reject bad seeds. They continually yield to the Holy Spirit. They have learned to discern between good and evil, thereby enabling them to produce 30, 60 or even 100-fold return.

CULTIVATED GROUND, CULTIVATED MIND

Just as Jesus compared people to types of soil, the human mind can be likened to a garden plot or farmer's field. The first year a garden or field is planted, many weed seeds in the soil sprout alongside the desired crop. Through constant cultivation, the gardener slowly diminishes the number of weeds in the soil. By killing the weeds, next season's weed seed potential is greatly limited. If the gardener continues to cultivate in the same area season after season, very few weed seeds will be left to sprout.

Although major reductions to weed activity are made in that area, winds and birds may drop a few surprises on the soil. Similarly, as we allow the Holy Spirit to reveal and deal with our attitudes, mindsets and thoughts, we produce a mind cultivated by the power of the Word of God. It is essential to understand, that we are continually weeding the garden of our minds and will ultimately put on the mind of Christ.

"And do not be conformed to this world, but be transformed by the renewing of your mind, that

you may prove what is that good and acceptable
and perfect will of God." (Romans 12:2)

SOURCE OF WATER, SOURCE OF THOUGHTS

The thoughts we choose to think are like the water poured upon the soil of our minds (2 Corinthians 10:5; 1 Corinthians 9:27). These thoughts determine the purity and productivity of the soil. There are three sources of natural water that convey this spiritual principle: irrigation water, rainwater, and well water.

IRRIGATION WATER

This water flows into a freshly cultivated field through an open canal, thereby collecting weed seeds. The more water that is allowed to enter, the greater the contamination. This can be compared to human thoughts that come by exposure to the world around us—both that which we choose to meditate on and that which we passively let in. They are a mixture of pure and impure. We can cultivate the human mind and eradicate weed seeds, but if we allow our minds to be watered with "canal water" (pure and impure thoughts) we will contaminate our cultivated and clean minds. What we expose ourselves to impacts our hearts. The world offers much mixture so we must guard our own hearts with all diligence, for out of it comes the issues of life (Proverbs 4:23).

Rain From Heaven

This is pure water that still contains a trace amount of atmospheric contamination. Receiving water this way sprouts whatever is in the ground. Furthermore, the gardener/farmer is dependent on the weather and, therefore, has no control over the flow. It is comparable to living one's life from one divinely inspired revelation to the next with no thought control between.

Well Water From God's Reservoirs and Underground Rivers

> *"He who believes in Me, as the Scripture has said,*
> *out of his heart will flow rivers of living water."*
> *(John 7:38)*

The Christian's source of water (thoughts) is Christ within. Through prayer, praise and worship, and studying the Bible, we invite God's presence, power and anointing to act as the electric power of the pump of faith. As we worship God and pray in our prayer language, we turn on the pump of faith and obedience. In this way, through the joy of the Holy Spirit, we draw from the well of life within us. This is the purest water for the thoughts of our mind—when we draw from the reservoirs within, we engage with God Himself:

> *"But You are holy, enthroned in the praises of Israel." (Psalm 22:3)*

> *"Serve the Lord with gladness; come before His presence with singing." (Psalm 100:2)*

> *"Therefore with joy you will draw water from the wells of salvation." (Isaiah 12:3)*

The basic biblical practice of renewing our mind and watering our souls with the presence of God's work helps to make us more effective ministers. As we receive from the Holy Spirit the call to minister to others, His Word will effectively pass through our own minds before we deliver it to others. Choosing to minister increases our responsibility to guard our own thoughts (hearts) with diligence. As we minister the compassionate heart of Jesus using our spiritual gifts, the words we share will reach, not just the ears, but the hearts of those to whom we are ministering. Our ministry will touch their very spirit by implanting and watering their own minds with thoughts from heaven. What an exciting reward that is!

6

The Revelation Gifts

"Therefore, brethren, desire earnestly to prophesy, and do not forbid to speak with tongues. Let all things be done decently and in order." 1 Corinthians 14:39-40

As we review the Bible and examine the characters who walked with God, we see that it was not just what was said that mattered, but how it was received and interpreted, as well. Many people could be in the same room and hear the same thing, but only a select few will receive the revelation of what was truly being communicated.

The revelation gifts function the same way: they reveal what was hidden in plain sight. In this chapter, we will define spiritual gifts and investigate, through Scripture, the revelation gifts of the Holy Spirit. The revelation gifts are just one of the three categories of the nine gifts of the spirit. The other categories, power and vocal gifts, function in similar principles as the revelation gifts. We focus on the revelation gifts as a key for effective ministry. Revelation gifts are divine revelation inspired by the Holy Spirit whereby the individual is permitted to see, understand, discern and perceive specific insight from the Lord's infinite knowledge and perspective.

WORD OF KNOWLEDGE

THREE TYPES OF KNOWLEDGE

Knowledge can be divided into three categories: human/natural, biblical/divine, and the word of knowledge (the gift of the Holy Spirit).

Human/natural knowledge or "sense knowledge" comes from the human soul and is gained by research and experience, for God has given individuals the power of creative thinking and learning. It is acquired by both the saved and unsaved.

True biblical/divine knowledge is based on revelation of the Scriptures from the Holy Spirit.[16] It is not simply memorizing the Bible or learning the "letter of the law," but involves receiving illumination from the Holy Spirit—the Word is rightly divided, alive, and applicable with proper doctrinal understanding.

The word of knowledge is the Holy Spirit gifting— it is an operation of the gift of the Holy Spirit within an individual. The individual receives and expresses this inspired knowledge by faith. It is an expression of the heart of God, not the reasoning of man, for the growth and establishment of His Church. It is beyond the natural; it is of God's higher thoughts and ways.

UNDERSTANDING THE WORD OF KNOWLEDGE

The word of knowledge is the supernatural revelation given by the Holy Spirit to a believer about specific facts in the mind of God for another—facts that are accurate and may give information about a person's past, present, or future. It is a word from God's infinite knowledge about the Earth, humanity and the universe. It is a glimpse of God's knowledge for a particular season or time, for a particular purpose, or for a need at a particular place. The gifting is not a gift of natural knowledge, nor a God-sent amplification of human knowledge. It is not intellectual capability, nor is it knowledge of the Word of God based on study. It is not an earned acquisition but a gift received by revelation instead of learning. Because a word of knowledge has the ability to penetrate through all human facades and pretenses, it is very helpful in counseling and witnessing. The word of knowledge delivered in due season goes straight to the heart and opens a door for God to minister.

BIBLICAL EXAMPLES OF THE WORD OF KNOWLEDGE

In 1 Samuel 9 and 10, Saul's father's donkeys were lost, so Saul inquired of Samuel, a prophet. Before Saul arrived at his house, Samuel received a word from God that he was to anoint Saul as king over Israel (9:16). When Saul arrived, Samuel gave him much information and insight by the word of knowledge and also anointed him king. After Saul was anointed (10:1-8), Saul hid. The Lord revealed where Saul was hiding by a word of knowledge (10:21-22).

In 1 Kings 14:2-3, Jeroboam's wife, the queen, disguised herself to see the blind prophet, Abijah. As she approached Abijah's house, the Lord gave him a word of knowledge (14:5). The word revealed her disguise.

In 1 Kings 5:20-27, Naaman came to Elisha for healing. Elisha told him by a word of knowledge to wash in the Jordan River seven times. Naaman obeyed and was healed and offered Elisha a great financial reward (14-15). Elisha refused, but his servant Gehazi secretly chased after Naaman to receive the reward for himself (19-23). The servant returned to his house and hid it. When Gehazi appeared before Elisha, Elisha asked, "Where have you been?" Gehazi lied saying, "I did not go anywhere." But Elisha, by the word of knowledge, revealed Gehazi's sin and pronounced the judgment of leprosy upon him and his descendants.

In John 4:17-29, Jesus met a Samaritan woman at a well and told her, by word of knowledge (4:17), her marriage history and current situation. Her amazement at one word of knowledge brought the whole city to the well and many were saved. This is the power of this gifting and the reason why God wants *all* Saints to be moving in all nine gifts!

In 2 Kings 6:8-12, the King of Aram was at war with Israel. Time and again he tried to set his camp in varying locations, but each time, the prophet Elisha warned the Israelites of the location; they prepared and were saved. The enraged King of Aram then called his servants together and asked which one was a spy for Israel! They replied:

> *"And one of his servants said, 'None, my lord, O king; but Elisha, the prophet who is in Israel, tells the king of Israel the words that you speak in your bedroom.'" (2 Kings 6:12)*

Israel was victorious through the word of knowledge and defeated their enemy.

As powerful as this revelation was in Old Testament times, the least of us in the Saints Movement will demonstrate Christ's Kingdom and will be able to do as much as the prophets in the Old Testament! Awake and arise saints! Prepare ye the way of the Lord!

In John 1:47-48, Jesus received a word of knowledge about Nathanael that revealed his location and the condition of his heart. Jesus stated by word of knowledge, "Here is a true Israelite, in whom there is nothing false" (v. 47). He also stated, "I saw you while you were still under the fig tree before Philip called you" (v. 48). Nathanael believed that Jesus was the Son of God because He ministered a word of knowledge (v. 49). Jesus could have chosen to minister another way, but He pierced Nathanael's heart with the word of knowledge and changed his life forever.

In Acts 5:1-11, Peter received a word of knowledge concerning a business transaction between Ananias and Sapphira. They came to church with the intention of lying in order to withhold a portion of their offering. The Lord exposed their wicked hearts to Peter, who said, "What made you think of doing such a thing? You have not lied to men but to God." God's immediate judgment was pronounced, and they both died instantly. This powerful demonstration of the word of knowledge purged the church of corruption and deception. It established a reverence for God, holiness, and truth in the Church's birth and foundation.

Peter, by word of knowledge, knew that three men were seeking him. By a word of wisdom, he was told what to do: "While Peter thought about the vision, the Spirit said to him, 'Behold, three men are seeking you'"

(Acts 10:19). There are these and many more examples of the word of knowledge in Scriptures.[17]

How Does the Word of Knowledge Operate?

The word of knowledge often operates during prophetic utterances:

> *"But if all prophesy, and an unbeliever or an uninformed person comes in, he is convinced by all, he is convicted by all. And thus, the secrets of his heart are revealed; and so, falling down on his face, he will worship God and report that God is truly among you." (1 Corinthians 14:24-25)*

Like all gifts of the Spirit, the word of knowledge should first be motivated by the Spirit. 1 Corinthians 12-14 demonstrates that love is the foundation for operating the word of knowledge. Just as Jesus was moved by compassion to heal the sick, we can be moved by love, by the Holy Spirit's leading, or by the desire to reveal Jesus to others to operate this gift.

We next activate the gift of the word of knowledge by our own faith. There is no need to wonder whether God wants to reveal Himself in this way; our faith in what Scripture has shown us gives us the confidence that He desires us to use this gift.

Finally, in love and faith, we minister the gift by obedience to the Word of God. This means that how we manage it is in agreement with Scripture. We develop the gift continually by "reason of use" (practice, practice, practice!) and expect to grow in our ability to use the gift. Discovering how His voice resounds in us comes by reason of use—the more we activate the gift, the more we will recognize it!

The Purpose of the Word of Knowledge

The word of knowledge is accurate information given through the Holy Spirit. It produces remarkable results that ultimately reveal Jesus and build the Kingdom of God. The following are examples of how the word of knowledge could be used to serve others:

- To reveal the cause of sickness or demonic possession.
- To reveal God's divine place for meetings (for example, the Last Supper).
- To reveal root problems in counseling.
- To reveal secrets of men's hearts so that repentance comes.
- To give insight into peoples' lives for intercessory prayer.
- To reveal lost persons or property.

The word of knowledge can reveal information that is detailed and potentially sensitive. The information is never to cause harm, but should rather reveal Jesus. Furthermore, it is not meant to serve our ambitions. Do not use the gifts of the Spirit to gain material wealth or prestige. Make sure your motives are pure when giving or receiving a gift. The gifts are not to be bought or sold.

WORD OF WISDOM

The word of wisdom is the supernatural ability in the Spirit to impart special and specific insight, instruction, guidance, or counsel. It brings life-changing illumination and course-changing decisions when heeded. It often brings the response, "What made you think of that? That is the very thing I needed to hear!" or, "Thanks to that word, my problem is solved!" When you are unaware of giftings operating in your life, you may also wonder, "What made me think of that?" It is not a gift of wisdom such as Solomon had. It is not insight gained through life's experiences, nor is it making the right decision based upon past education, training or events. It is a gift of a revelation of wisdom supernaturally given by God.

Similarly to knowledge, we can look at wisdom in three categories: natural/worldly wisdom, biblical/divine wisdom, and the gift of the word of wisdom.

Natural or Worldly Wisdom

The first level of wisdom, natural wisdom, is the application of human knowledge. Man's wisdom is evident in his ability to bring forth creative inventions, such as airplanes, spaceships, weapons of war, computer technology, and mobile phones. Natural wisdom is valuable, but in itself does not lead to the Kingdom of God:

> *"Where is the wise? Where is the scribe? Where is the disputer of this age? Has not God made foolish the wisdom of this world? For Jews request a sign, and Greeks seek after wisdom. But God has chosen the foolish things of the world to put to shame the wise, and God has chosen the weak things of the world to put to shame the things which are mighty." (1 Corinthians 1:20, 22, 27)*

Paul emphasized that salvation is not gained by worldly wisdom, which the Greeks sought after, but that God uses the foolishness of preaching. 1 Corinthians 2:1 reinforces this when Paul said, "And I, brethren, when I came to you, did not come with excellence of speech or of wisdom declaring to you the testimony of God." He understood that supernatural demonstration was more convincing than eloquent sermons. He wanted their faith to rest in God's power, not in human wisdom.

King Solomon is our example of one of the wisest men in history, and he is where we get much of our Scriptures on wisdom. He attained all possible worldly goods in the form of wealth, success, and authority, but said: "Then I saw that wisdom excels folly as light excels darkness" (Ecclesiastes 2:13). Solomon reveals that pursuing "wisdom concerning all things that are done under heaven" is vanity (Ecclesiastes 1:2; 2:11; 12:12-13)—this shows us that natural wisdom is least of all.

BIBLICAL OR DIVINE WISDOM

The second level of wisdom is biblical or divine wisdom. Paul compares natural wisdom and biblical wisdom in 1 Corinthians 2:7, 13:

> *"But we speak the wisdom of God in a mystery, the hidden wisdom which God ordained before the ages for our glory. These things we also speak, not in words which man's wisdom teaches but which the Holy Spirit teaches, comparing spiritual things with spiritual."*

The difference between natural wisdom and biblical wisdom is that biblical wisdom has its source in God. Psalm 111:10 says that the beginning of wisdom is the fear of the Lord. Wisdom comes from God and His Word taken to heart; prayerful study and meditation increase this wisdom. The following are insightful Scriptures on this mature Christian wisdom:

> *"Wisdom is better than strength... The words of wise men are heard in quiet... Wisdom is better than weapons of war..." (Ecclesiastes 9:16-18)*

> *"That the God of our Lord Jesus Christ, the Father of glory, may give unto you the spirit of wisdom and revelation in the knowledge of him: The eyes of your understanding being enlightened; that ye may know what is the hope of his calling, and what the riches of the glory of his inheritance in the saints." (Ephesians 1:17-18)*

> *"There shall come forth a Rod from the stem of Jesse, and a Branch shall grow out of his roots. The Spirit of the Lord shall rest upon Him, the Spirit of wisdom and understanding, the Spirit of counsel and might, the Spirit of knowledge and of the fear of the Lord." (Isaiah 11:1-2)*

> *"But of Him you are in Christ Jesus, who became for us wisdom from God—and righteousness and sanctification and redemption." (1 Corinthians 1:30)*

"So you shall speak to all who are gifted artisans, whom I have filled with the spirit of wisdom..."
(Exodus 28:3)

"Behold, the fear of the Lord, that is wisdom..."
(Job 28:28)

"Wisdom is found on the lips of him who has understanding. But a man of understanding has wisdom." (Proverbs 10:13, 23)

"When pride comes, then comes shame; but with the humble is wisdom." (Proverbs 11:2)

"By pride comes nothing but strife, but with the well-advised is wisdom." (Proverbs 13:10)

"Why is there in the hand of a fool the purchase price of wisdom, since he has no heart for it?"
(Proverbs 17:16)

"Who is wise and understanding among you? Let him show by good conduct that his works are done in the meekness of wisdom. But if you have bitter envy and self-seeking in your hearts, do not boast and lie against the truth. This wisdom does not descend from above, but is earthly, sensual,

> *demonic. For where envy and self-seeking exist,*
> *confusion and every evil thing are there. But*
> *the wisdom that is from above is first pure, then*
> *peaceable, gentle, willing to yield, full of mercy*
> *and good fruits, without partiality and without*
> *hypocrisy. Now the fruit of righteousness is sown in*
> *peace by those who make peace." (James 3:13–18)*

Biblical wisdom is not given by default—we must ask for it and develop it through biblical principles. An individual can move in all the gifts of the Spirit and not have mature Christian wisdom. Spirituality and maturity are not the same. Maturity is Christian character, integrity and meekness before God. Spirituality as relating to using the gifts comes by faith.

THE HOLY SPIRIT GIFT OF THE WORD OF WISDOM

The third level of wisdom is the word of wisdom. This gift of Holy Spirit is described in 1 Corinthians 12:1-3:

> *"Now concerning spiritual gifts, brethren, I do*
> *not want you to be ignorant: You know that you*
> *were Gentiles, carried away to these dumb idols,*
> *however you were led. Therefore I make known to*
> *you that no one speaking by the Spirit of God calls*
> *Jesus accursed, and no one can say that Jesus is*
> *Lord except by the Holy Spirit."*

This is God-given wisdom that has futuristic application for people, things, or events. In this case, the word of wisdom tells us how to take action regarding the recently revealed facts, or word of knowledge. It is the heart of God giving strategy, insight, or plans that have not been spoken of or written. It is not revelation of His written Word, nor is it anything that contradicts it.

BIBLICAL EXAMPLES OF THE WORD OF WISDOM

In Genesis 41, Joseph interpreted both of Pharaoh's dreams by word of wisdom. He needed revelation from God in order to perceive the true interpretation. By a word of wisdom, Joseph warned Pharaoh of the seven-year famine.

In Exodus 3, Moses needed a word of wisdom many times while leading the children of Israel out of Egypt. Moses had a word of wisdom when he dealt with Pharaoh and said, "Let my people go."

In 1 Kings 3:16-28, Solomon, by word of wisdom, ruled in the case of the two mothers and one child; he administered justice by revealing to whom the child belonged. The child was spared, and the true mother was vindicated.

In Genesis 6:14-18, by word of wisdom, Noah was forewarned to build an ark in order to save his family from God's impending judgment.

In Genesis 19, Lot was warned of the coming destruction of Sodom.

In Exodus 34-40, Moses received instructions from God on how to build the Tabernacle and organize the tribes of Israel.

In Acts 27:21-25, during a storm, Paul told the crew what to do and encouraged them that all of them would survive.

The word of wisdom is useful in providing instruction and strategy, even when there appears to be no logical explanation:

> *"However, when He, the Spirit of truth, has come, He will guide you into all truth; for He will not speak on His own authority, but whatever He hears He will speak; and He will tell you things to come." (John 16:13)*

How the Word of Wisdom Operates

All gifts are motivated by the Holy Spirit and activated by the individual's faith. The word of wisdom can be a flash of revelation or insight. It can manifest as a vision, a slight mental impression, or can come through a prophetic flow. It is not human reasoning. Human reasoning can hinder an individual from receiving divine revelation. The two are totally different! Like all gifts, the individual only learns by exercising the gift.

Purpose of the Word of Wisdom

All the revelation gifts help us see Christ Jesus and His operation in us, through us to others, and to build the Kingdom. They are to serve others for His glory. The following are ways in which the word of wisdom serves others:

- To warn of impending danger.
- To make known or confirm a ministry call.
- To give assurance of blessing to come.
- To warn of judgment to come.
- To give instruction on how things are to be done God's way.
- To give insight and understanding that will advance His cause, others and you.

The word of wisdom builds people in order to build the Kingdom. One place this gift is quite strategic and necessary is in the marketplace. Marketplace ministry will be the new frontier for Kingdom advancement in the Saints Movement. (Read more about this in my book, *The Day of the Saints - Equipping Believers for Their Revolutionary Role in Ministry*.)

DISCERNING OF SPIRITS

A precise definition of discerning of spirits is challenging because this gift is only mentioned once in the Bible. However, by taking into account what the Scriptures say about spirits and applying some word study, we can gain an understanding of this gift. "Discerning of spirits" implies the supernatural ability to discern which spirit is motivating human words and behaviors. It is a sense by the Holy Spirit into the spirit realm. There are three sources of spirits: human, satanic, and godly. Corinthians and John both show us this:

> *"Therefore I make known to you that no one speaking by the Spirit of God calls Jesus accursed, and no one can say that Jesus is Lord except by the Holy Spirit." (1 Corinthians 12:3)*

> *"Beloved, do not believe every spirit, but test the spirits, whether they are of God; because many false prophets have gone out into the world." (1 John 4:1)*

We can understand discerning of spirits as both general and specific. Discerning of spirits can generally be defined as: determination of the "spiritual source" of a word, attitude, individual action, atmosphere, or corporate environment. In this general sense, the operation of the gift of discerning of spirits helps to determine whether something is of divine, devilish, or human origin. The Bible refers to these three sources: the Word of God (1 Peter 1:23-25), the doctrine and traditions of men (Colossians 2:22), and the doctrine of demons

(1 Timothy 4:1). This is similar to how the Bible differentiates between the wisdom of God (1 Corinthians 1:30), the wisdom of man (1 Corinthians 1:20; 2:4-5), and the counsel of the ungodly (Psalm 1:1; James 3:15). In its most basic application, discerning of spirits helps us identify which of these three sources are at work in any given situation. However, discerning of spirits can also be more specific. This gift can give us the ability to identify specific evil spirits and their devices.[18] Therefore, discerning of spirits is a safeguard against deception.[19]

The Greek word for "discerning" *diakrisis*, meaning "judging through." The concept in the Greek context refers to piercing of all that is outward and seeing right through; this implies clear vision, clear understanding, and a supernatural perceptiveness. The gift is not a keen insight into human nature by reasoning, logic, common sense, experience or trained analysis. It also is not an evaluation based on what is seen in personality, character, physical features, nationality, body language, personality types, or facial expression.

THREE LEVELS OF DISCERNING

There are three levels of discerning of spirits: natural, psychic, and divine gifting.

Natural discernment is built into our instincts through learning, and to some degree, all of us utilize this level. Anyone who interacts with people can develop natural discernment and perception through observing actions, words and mannerisms. This is what people are often referring to when they say they can "read people," or "read the room"—it can also simply be a sense of internal workings based on outward signals like body language. Classes and training may enable one to evaluate people more effectively.

Psychic discernment, on the other hand, is a counterfeit to God's intended spiritual gifts. Man was created in God's image as a creative being with spiritual desires and discernment. These can be developed with the tremendous mental capacity given to man. The human mind has great power and when given over to the realm of spiritual darkness, in embracing that which is not of God, a "gate of hell" is opened. Psychic discernment may employ the use of demonic influence.

The supernatural, Holy Spirit gift of discernment is the third level of discerning. The divine gift of discernment is the God-given ability, by the "eye of the Holy Spirit," to see into the three realms of the spirit: the kingdom of darkness, the kingdom of light, and the human spirit (Colossians 1:13). The Holy Spirit communicates the motive or origin of an action, attitude, or atmosphere. With it we can discern (detect) the Lord's divine leading and presence. We can recognize demonic activity in people or over geographical locations, or discern human motives that would cause a person to act or think a certain way.

BIBLICAL EXAMPLES OF DISCERNMENT

Mark 9:17 says, "Then one of the crowds answered and said, 'Teacher, I brought You my son, who has a mute spirit.'" A father brought his boy to Jesus and His disciples in search of deliverance for his son. Jesus used discerning of spirits to determine that it was a deaf and dumb spirit and then proceeded to deliver the boy. Note that Jesus did not succumb to His natural senses. He could have thought the boy was possessed with a suicidal spirit, a self-destructive spirit, or even an epileptic spirit because of the erratic way the boy acted.

In Matthew 16:15-23, Jesus rebuked Peter for denying He was going to die. Jesus discerned Peter was speaking from the wrong spirit and said, "Get behind me, Satan! You are an offense to me, for you are not mindful of the things of God, but the things of men."

In Acts 8:23, Peter discerned that Simon's motives were wrong when he asked for the Holy Spirit. Asking to receive the Holy Spirit obviously seems like a good thing, but because Peter discerned, he was aware that this request was not one for him to minister to.

In Acts 13:9-12, the Holy Spirit revealed to Paul that Barjesus was a child of the devil and opposed everything upright. Paul spoke judgment against him, and he was blind for a season.

In Acts 16:16-18, Paul rebuked a woman at Philippi after he discerned that she was possessed with a spirit of divination.

THE GIFT OF DISCERNING OF SPIRITS

As we have seen with each of the gifts, discerning of spirits is motivated by the Holy Spirit and activated by an individual's faith! It can come as a flash of revelation in our thoughts, as a vision, or as a slight mental impression or prophetic flow. It is not human reasoning but Holy Spirit-inspired revelation. It can come as an inner alert as the spirit realm affects our physical senses. Hebrews 5:14 says we have our senses exercised to know (discern) both good and evil.

Never attribute critical or judgmental thinking to this gifting. God's purpose for the gift is to reveal Jesus and bring redemption and restoration. The Lord does not sanction faultfinding, or "detectives" looking to point blame or guilt—He does not look favorably on those who operate out of divisive and unloving hearts.

THE PURPOSE OF DISCERNING OF SPIRITS

This powerful revelatory gift can bring clarity, safety and freedom in individuals, groups and regions. When operating healthily in the believer the gift is useful:

- To reveal demonic principalities and powers over geographical areas. Prayer prepares the way for the advancement of the Kingdom. This gift illuminates what to pray.
- To reveal specific demonic spirits that are hindering or possessing people. (Word of knowledge may reveal the circumstances and time when a demonic spirit enters into someone, but discerning of spirits reveals what type of spirit is present.)
- To reveal what is in an individual's human spirit that would cause them to say something or act in a particular manner. This revelation could help the believer become free and healed.
- To reveal the direction and flow that the Holy Spirit has for a service or group, such as a spirit of worship, spirit of praise, spirit of intercession, and spirit of joy.

Regardless of the specific thing discerned or revealed, the ultimate purpose is always the Kingdom of God. In other words, the use of the gift can help bring righteousness, peace and joy.

7

The Keys to the Kingdom

"Having then gifts differing according to the grace that is given to us, let us use them: if prophecy, let us prophesy in proportion to our faith." Romans 12:6

Using the gifts of the Holy Spirit is both an honor and a command, but it never needs to be a burden. In fact, ministering the gifts of the Holy Spirit is a joy! To use them diligently, God has given us tremendous keys so we can experience first-hand that His burden is light. As we explore the power of the Kingdom and the keys that have been given to the church, we will discover the ability God has given to man to walk in prosperity, the potential God has given man to become all that he can be, and the identity God has placed in man to manifest the Kingdom of God within the Earth.

In this chapter, we will discuss the seven keys God has given us to operate in His Kingdom: gaining knowledge and understanding; believing in faith; having grace; praying in the Spirit; accessing joy and praise; reason of use; and being made an able minister. These keys not only bring us personal victory in our lives, but also help us minister in prophecy and use all the gifts of the Holy Spirit.

THE KEY OF KNOWLEDGE AND UNDERSTANDING

BIBLICAL KNOWLEDGE

To gain the key of knowledge and understanding, we must first hear the truth—for the truth sets us free to operate in all that God has for us. Psalm 119:130 says, "The entrance of Your words gives light; it gives understanding to the simple." Hearing the Word of God brings knowledge to our soul and enlightens the dark areas of our being: "If you abide in My word, you are My disciples indeed. And you shall know the truth, and the truth shall make you free" (John 8:31-32).

Knowledge and understanding begin with Scriptures. Building knowledge of the Word sets the mind free to receive from God's Spirit. Biblical knowledge is the basis for all we do and manifest. As we build the knowledge of the Word of God into our hearts and minds, it opens, extends and clears communication lines—it allows God to speak into our lives. We can then hear what the Spirit is saying to us: "But the people who know their God shall be strong and carry out great exploits" (Daniel 11:32, Proverbs 6:23; 2 Peter 1:19).

EYES OF UNDERSTANDING BEING ENLIGHTENED

Gaining biblical knowledge is the first step, but our journey into knowledge and understanding does not stop with reading or memorizing Scripture. Something amazing happens beyond the logical meaning of the words we read on the pages of our Bible. The Holy Spirit is able to make Scriptures come alive to us by causing our eyes to be opened to receive the meaning:

> *"Do not cease to give thanks for you, making mention of you in my prayers: that the God of our Lord Jesus Christ, the Father of glory, may give to you the spirit of wisdom and revelation in the knowledge of Him, the eyes of your understanding being enlightened; that you may know what is the hope of His calling, what are the riches of the glory of His inheritance in the saints, and what is the exceeding greatness of His power toward us who*

believe, according to the working of His mighty
power." (Ephesians 1:16-19)

This revelation is much more impactful than our basic reading comprehension. In fact, plenty of scholars have studied the Scriptures without understanding their meaning and without ever coming to know Christ further. Therefore, having our eyes of understanding enlightened is critical to gain true biblical knowledge and understanding.

Growing in the knowledge of God and the Word, with a deepening love and reverence for Him, illuminates our mind to the mind of Christ. The prayer for the "spirit of wisdom and revelation" (Ephesians 1:17) is seeking insight into truths of God beyond the natural human ability to attain. The Word of Life becoming alive in us is an operation of the Holy Spirit in our new creation spirit-man. The soul (mind, will, emotions) receives from the spirit in man, and conveys it to the whole man: "'You shall not live by bread alone,' the Lord says, 'but every word that proceeds out of the mouth of God'" (Matthew 4:4). This revelation opens the window of the soul to the spirit realm.

FOUR HINDRANCES TO RECEIVING TRUTH

We can receive the truth as we read Scriptures and allow the Holy Spirit to open our eyes of understanding.

Still, it is possible to engage in Scriptures and prayer, and even in the presence of God, without receiving the truth of what Scriptures say. The following are four element that could potentially hinder us from truly receiving personal revelation of the truth.

1. A LACK OF UNDERSTANDING OF GOD'S VISION FOR HIS CHURCH.

If we do not know the history of where the Church has been, and where God's vision is to take Her, we can get stuck in today's understanding of present truth. We must understand historical restoration and progressive moves of God. Psalm 119:130 says: "The unfolding of your words gives light; it gives understanding to the simple" (NIV). God is accomplishing His Word unto "the restoration of all things" (Acts 3:21).

An example of how God is moving the Church into the restoration of truth is the preservation of the Bible during the Dark Ages—before salvation was taught as by faith. It was not until Martin Luther's 95 Thesis that the masses regained access to biblical truths that were always there but were simply unrevealed to that generation. Today, we continue to "gain access" to biblical truth that has perhaps been in front of us the entire time; we did not see it because it was hidden from our eyes of understanding. (My book *The Eternal Church* defines, precept upon precept, the unfolding of God's plan for the "restoration of all things" and the historical moves of God into the 21st century.)

2. An Unwillingness to Accept Truth When it is Heard.

The natural mind wars with the things of the Spirit (Romans 8). Receiving the truth is a choice—we may choose to be unwilling because we simply do not like what we hear. The truth may go against our desires or choices, and we may not want to give up those things. Furthermore, we may be unwilling to receive the truth because we fear it could cause pain. For example, a person whose child has entered into a homosexual lifestyle may not want to believe that God hates that lifestyle since they know that God loves their child. While both can be true simultaneously, the pain of knowing a child is actively living against God can feel like more than a person is willing to accept. In many cases, an unwillingness to accept the truth when we hear it can feel justified if we allow ourselves to hold on to our natural thinking rather than letting the sharpness of Scripture "divide between soul and spirit" (Hebrews 4:12).

3. Mindsets Ingrained by the "Doctrines of Men."

These mindsets hinder or prevent receiving the things that witness to their spirit man, though plainly written in the Scriptures. Psalm 19:8 says, "The statutes of the Lord are right, rejoicing the heart (a witness in the Spirit); the commandment of the Lord is pure, enlightening the eyes (gives spiritual eyesight to comprehend spiritual things)." We must go after and maintain our love for His Word. In our love and respect for the weight of His Living Word, our conscious mind can be set free to receive from His Spirit.

4. A LUKEWARM-NESS OR "CHILL" FOR THE THINGS OF GOD.

Second Thessalonians 2:10 says, "They perish because they refused to love the truth and so be saved" (NIV). Not loving truth allows us to be deceived. When we neglect to love truth, we risk using whatever we do love to justify a distortion of truth. If we do not love truth, we may be unwilling to suffer in pursuit of truth and the presence of God when persecution comes.

It is unlikely that we choose to read the Bible or receive biblical teaching with the intent to reject truth or be deceived. However, areas of our heart may allow us to accept deception by causing us to reject uncomfortable truth when we hear it—or justify why we are exempt from truths we have heard. By being aware of our potential resistance to truth, we can willfully keep our hearts soft and open and catch any inclination we have to not receive biblical knowledge and understanding.

THE KEY OF
IN FAITH BELIEVING

*"Having then gifts differing according to the grace
that is given to us, let us use them: if prophecy, let
us prophesy in proportion to our faith."*
Romans 12:6

FAITH AS ACTIVATOR AND KEY TO THE SPIRITUAL REALM

Faith is the only way to access the gifts. Faith acts as an activator or "door opener" and causes the spiritual realm to become a working reality. Matthew 9:29 says, "According to your faith be it unto you." Faith is acting on God's Word and will. Remember that God gives us faith and enables us to do what He has called us to do. The Word only profits those who mix it with faith. We must exercise what He has given. The more we activate and use our faith, the more God can do in us.[20]

THE HEART IS THE INNER MAN OR SPIRIT

Our natural human faith combined with faith in God gives us the divine faith of the Son of God. Romans 12:3 says, "God has dealt to each one a measure of faith." It is God's divine faith and heart that enables us to act, decide, do, speak, and minister the mind of Christ. When faith rises up to minister the mind of

God, it releases compassion to minister the heart of God—it touches and meets the deep needs of mankind. Out of the belly flows communication (rivers of living water) from the Spirit of God (John 7:38). These waters flow more richly and deeply with faith and exercise—they flow with the current in which the Holy Spirit moves. This is not based on our logical reasoning, but rather on trust and faith in an almighty, all-knowing God and His Word.

FAITH HAS NO EMOTION

Man is a three-part being: a spirit, a soul and a body. 1 Thessalonians 5:23 says this:

> *"Now may the God of peace Himself sanctify you completely; and may your whole spirit, soul, and body be preserved blameless at the coming of our Lord Jesus Christ."*

The soulish realm of man is comprised of the mind, will, and emotions—this includes feelings of anger, excitement, fear, depression and anxiety. The spirit of man, when born of God, is alive unto God. The new Spirit is to be given a place of dominance over the soulish realm of man's mind, will, and emotions. We do not have to wait for an emotional feeling to move in the gifts. The Spirit through faith activates them. Waiting for "a feeling" to confirm faith is a great way to invite intimidation. Faith is a fruit of the Spirit, not of the soul or of the flesh. This is why faith does not wait for a feeling—it acts:

> *"For assuredly, I say to you, whoever says to this mountain, 'Be removed and be cast into the sea,' and does not doubt in his heart, but believes that those things he says will be done, he will have whatever he say." (Mark 11:23)*

THE KEY OF BY GRACE

Grace is God's divine enablement. It is having God's supernatural ability to perform whatever He directs us to do. It is unearned. Through faith, good stewards minister by it:

> *"As each one has received a gift, minister it to one another, as good stewards of the manifold grace of God. If anyone speaks, let him speak as the oracles of God. If anyone ministers, let him do it as with the ability which God supplies, that in all things God may be glorified through Jesus Christ, to whom belong the glory and the dominion forever and ever. Amen." (1 Peter 4:10–11)*

The grace of God in ministry is that He wants to touch people through you as much as you do (if not more). He wants to do it and is only looking for someone willing. If you are the willing individual, who by faith takes action, His grace will accomplish what He wants through you.

GIFTS VS. FRUIT

The supernatural gifts are given while the fruit of the Spirit is grown. As 1 Corinthians 12:7 reveals, "the manifestation of the Spirit is given to each one." The gifts of the Spirit are given as a manifestation of the love of the Giver. This is a critical distinction to make. When a gift is given, it can be used immediately, regardless of the recipient's skill level. The instant we activate the gift of the Holy Spirit, we are ministering. There is no junior Holy Spirit. His gifts work. We must learn to use them with growing efficiency, but also understand that we can use them immediately without prior experience.

Fruit, on the other hand, is not given. It is sown, cultivated, grown and harvested. This means the fruit of the Holy Spirit, such as kindness, may not be well developed in a person with the gifts of the Holy Spirit, such as prophecy. In essence, an unkind person can prophesy an accurate ministry. Does God want both the gifts and the fruit to be developed? Of course. But that does not mean He prevents a person with little or poor fruit from ministering the gifts.

SPIRITUALITY VS. MATURITY

Since fruit must be grown over time, we must recognize that a demonstration of the gifts does not reflect the fruit or character of the person demonstrating them. Gifts can be manifest instantly—a person may seem spiritual because they can use a gift of the Spirit, but that same person could be immature in their character, knowledge of Scripture, or fruit of the Spirit. Spiritual gifts are never contingent on maturity or character. Therefore, it is up to believers to recognize the difference between spiritual gifts and Godly character, and choose to let God develop the character needed to become Christlike.

We are commanded to "follow after charity" or "pursue love," which is the divine nature of God: "pursue love, and desire spiritual gifts, but especially that you may prophesy," (1 Corinthians 14:1). God is love. We must grow in Christ-like love, which cannot be imparted by the laying on of hands. It is only through God's processes that Christlike nature can develop in us. God is looking at our ability to change as a result of allowing His nature to develop in us: "Because they do not change, therefore they do not fear God" (Psalm 55:19). He is looking for us to be changed into the likeness of Christ, from glory to glory—not just our ability to use the gifts of the Spirit:

> *"But we all, with unveiled face, beholding as in a mirror the glory of the Lord, are being transformed into the same image from glory to glory, just as by the Spirit of the Lord." (2 Corinthians 3:18)*

We are to "desire spiritual gifts." The spirituality of the gifts, manifested by grace and obedience, is not based on how much we know or how mature we are—it is based upon a desire to speak the heart and mind of God to others. Romans 12:1-21 (NIV) relates a several fundamental keys to manifesting the gifts based on faith, grace, and continued growth into maturity. Verses 1-3 reveal how to begin to move in the gifts:

> *"Therefore, I urge you, brothers and sisters, in view of God's mercy, to offer your bodies as a living sacrifice, holy and pleasing to God—this is your true and proper worship. Do not conform to the pattern of this world, but be transformed by the renewing of your mind. Then you will be able to test and approve what God's will is—his good, pleasing and perfect will. For by the grace given me I say to every one of you: Do not think*

> *of yourself more highly than you ought, but*
> *rather think of yourself with sober judgment, in*
> *accordance with the faith God has distributed to*
> *each of you."*

Verses 4-8 tell the believer what to do with the gifts:

> *"For just as each of us has one body with many*
> *members, and these members do not all have the*
> *same function, so in Christ we, though many,*
> *form one body, and each member belongs to all*
> *the others. We have different gifts, according*
> *to the grace given to each of us. If your gift is*
> *prophesying, then prophesy in accordance with*
> *your faith; if it is serving, then serve; if it is*
> *teaching, then teach; if it is to encourage, then*
> *give encouragement; if it is giving, then give*
> *generously; if it is to lead, do it diligently; if it is*
> *to show mercy, do it cheerfully."*

Verses 9-21 relate to the believer how to keep pure and in the right attitude and perspective, and how to operate maturely:

> *"Love must be sincere. Hate what is evil; cling to*
> *what is good. Be devoted to one another in love.*
> *Honor one another above yourselves. Never be*

*lacking in zeal, but keep your spiritual fervor,
serving the Lord. Be joyful in hope, patient in
affliction, faithful in prayer. Share with the Lord's
people who are in need. Practice hospitality. Bless
those who persecute you; bless and do not curse.
Rejoice with those who rejoice; mourn with those
who mourn. Live in harmony with one another.
Do not be proud, but be willing to associate with
people of low position. Do not be conceited. Do not
repay anyone evil for evil. Be careful to do what is
right in the eyes of everyone. If it is possible, as far
as it depends on you, live at peace with everyone.
Do not take revenge, my dear friends, but leave
room for God's wrath, for it is written: 'It is mine
to avenge; I will repay,' says the Lord. On the
contrary: 'If your enemy is hungry, feed him; if he is
thirsty, give him something to drink. In doing this,
you will heap burning coals on his head.' Do not be
overcome by evil, but overcome evil with good."*

Spirituality gives us instant access to the gifts. Maturity causes us to utilize them with the heart of God and to the fullness of His purpose.

IDEAL VS. REAL

Many saints believe that a Christian must be 100% perfect in every area of their lives before they can move in ministering the Holy Spirit's gifts. If this were true, *no one would be able to move in the gifts!* The reality is that God's grace and undeserved favor is sufficient. We are the best that God has! If He cannot work with imperfect people, He will have no one to work with.

The Lord teaches us to continue to grow up and become holy, but activating the gifts requires only two prerequisites: faith and grace. Therefore, demonstrating the gifts does not verify or confirm our moral uprightness, doctrinal accuracy, or business integrity! The use of the gifts is not based on the believer's maturity, but upon what Jesus has already done. They are free gifts, not earned by merit.

Consider the Corinthian church in their gross carnality—even they had great manifestations of the gifts. They had so many gifts in operation that Paul had to give them constructive guidelines about how to operate the gifts in a corporate assembly. Consider the following questions:

- Was the Church at Corinth experiencing doctrinal problems? (1 Corinthians 11:19; 2 Corinthians 11)
- Were they experiencing carnality? Were they experiencing moral failures and problems? (1 Corinthians 3:3. 5:1. 6:1)
- Were they zealously desiring, pursuing, and operating in the gifts?

God used the Church at Corinth to be the biblical example for all future believers to learn about using the gifts of the Holy Spirit. The fact that they could learn in front of us, with us knowing their struggles, shows us that God wants us to learn to demonstrate His gifts even as we work out our salvation.

THE KEY OF PRAYING IN THE SPIRIT

"He who speaks in a tongue edifies himself."
1 Corinthians 14:4

Praying in the Holy Spirit with your prayer language, the gift of tongues, is a powerful gift that helps us in many ways and edifies us personally—it serves in ministering the other spiritual gifts. It gives us power and builds us up:

"But you shall receive power when the Holy Spirit
has come upon you; and you shall be witnesses."
(Acts 1:8)

"But you, beloved, building yourselves up on your
most holy faith, praying in the Holy Spirit, keep
yourselves in the love of God, looking for the mercy of
our Lord Jesus Christ unto eternal life." (Jude 20:21)

The gift of tongues is so beneficial, in fact, that I wrote *78 Reasons for Praying in Tongues* to inspire believers of the incredible value in this gift.

PRAYING IN THE SPIRIT—A POWER GENERATOR

The Holy Spirit uses the born-again, Spirit-filled believer's ability to pray in the Spirit as a power generator. As we pray in the Spirit, the Holy Spirit uses tongues to generate that power. Think of it like an engine—an engine is full of power, but to get it started, you use a "starter" (essentially a much smaller motor) to turn over the engine until its own power takes effect. Praying in the Spirit acts as a "starter" (a faith action), which activates the mighty power of the Holy Spirit. Praying in the Spirit stirs up our spirits and spiritual gifts, so they can begin to operate at their full power.

PRAYING IN THE SPIRIT ENABLES THE SAINTS

Our spiritual abilities do not come from our bodies or our brains—they come from the Spirit and must function by the Spirit. Remember, we are spirit beings living in a body. Sometimes we feel that our natural world and natural senses are predominant, but in fact, the more "real" reality is, the more dominant the reality of the spirit realm.

Praying in the Spirit engages us in the reality of the Kingdom of God to a greater degree. As Zechariah 4:6 proclaims, "'[It is] not by might nor by power, but by My Spirit,' says the Lord of hosts." Praying in the Spirit enables the believer to minister the mind of Christ and enables them to receive pure thoughts from the throne of God. It also allows us to activate the other eight gifts of the Spirit (1 Corinthians 12:8-10) and helps us move into our membership ministry in the Body of Christ by manifest mighty miracles. (Refer to *The Day of the Saints* for our membership ministry.)

THE KEY OF
JOY AND PRAISE

"Therefore with joy you will draw water from the wells of salvation." Isaiah 12:3

Joy as a Power Switch to Release the Mind of Christ

Joy is the bucket to draw out of the wells of salvation. Joy acts like a faucet handle. We engage joy in order to release the mind of Christ (water) which is deposited in our redeemed spirit (the well). A natural correlation is oil or water hidden deep underground. To draw out the resources, one must drill through layers of soil. This can be compared to allowing the Word of God to drill through our fears, anxieties, feelings of unworthiness, doubts or erroneous doctrine. Our faith is planted more firmly with each hardened layer we confront and conquer. Once the source is tapped, Joy acts as the pump to our redeemed human spirit—it draws the mind of Christ up and out so that others are blessed.

PRAISE AS A SPIRITUAL FORCE TO CLEAR THE MIND

God inhabits the praises of His people and our praise ushers in the presence of God. His presence brings life and allows His thoughts to be released. Divine joy, life of Christ, and divine thoughts flow from the Holy Spirit into the spirit of man and flood the conscious mind. According to Isaiah 40:31, there is even a refreshing that rejuvenates the natural body:

> *"But those who wait on the Lord shall renew their strength; they shall mount up with wings like eagles, they shall run and not be weary, they shall walk and not faint but they that wait upon the Lord shall renew their strength; they shall mount up with wings as eagles; they shall run, and not be weary; and they shall walk, and not faint."*

Praise causes God to arise and inhabit our praises. Scripture tells us to let God arise and His enemies be scattered (Psalm 68:1). When we praise, such as celebration and shouting, not only does God's presence come, but any other presence scatters. How much better the environment for ministry is when we praise![21]

THE KEY OF "BY REASON OF USE"

Skilled Ability to Function in Our Gift Comes by Doing

We only gain ability by doing. If an attorney can practice law, a doctor can practice medicine, and our worship leader can practice with the worship team, then we can practice the presence of the Lord! Practice exercises our spiritual senses so they will grow: "But solid food belongs to those who are of full age, that is, those who by reason of use have their senses exercised to discern both good and evil" (Hebrews 5:14).

We only grow in our spiritual abilities by continually exercising our spiritual senses. You must begin to operate in it for it to grow.

Doing the Word Brings Us into Heart-Level Knowing

Our willingness to obey God demonstrates to Him our willing heart and faith in Him. It demonstrates to us His faithfulness, love, truth and power. It demonstrates to others what we believe in our hearts and His Lord-ship. Furthermore, in doing the actions that we know to do (such as using our gifts), we are helped to not become deceived: "But be doers of the word, and not hearers only, deceiving yourselves" (James 1:22).

Determining to do what God asks of us sets us up to discern His will better: "If anyone wills to do His will, he shall know concerning the doctrine, whether it is from God or whether I speak on My own authority" (John 7:17).

It also brings us into the Kingdom of God: "Not everyone who says to Me, 'Lord, Lord,' shall enter the kingdom of heaven, but he who does the will of My Father in heaven" (Matthew 7:21).

In these ways, taking action changes us from having just intellectual knowledge to knowing with our whole being: "Let us know, let us pursue the knowledge of the Lord" (Hosea 6:3).

We Only Believe What We Act Upon

The believer must act on current revelation the Father reveals. If we do not act upon it, then do we believe it? The one who is casual in his responses may not re-ceive much, but the one who acts on what God reveals will receive more revelation. God desires a whole heart, zealous unto good works:

"Thus also faith by itself, if it does not have works (no action), is dead. But someone will say, you have faith, and I have works. Show me your faith without your works, and I will show you my faith by my works. Do you see that faith was working together with his works, and by works faith was made perfect? You see then that a man is justified by works, and not by faith only. For as the body without the spirit is dead, so faith without works (the working of your faith) is dead also." (James 2:17-26, emphasis added)

Taking action is the key to our fully believing and our faith coming alive.

THE KEY OF ALL BEING MADE ABLE MINISTERS

"And He Himself gave some to be apostles, some prophets, some evangelists, and some pastors and teachers, for the equipping of the saints for the work of ministry, for the edifying of the body of Christ." Ephesians 4:11-12

FIVE-FOLD MINISTERS ARE CALLED TO BRING THE SAINTS INTO THEIR MEMBERSHIP MINISTRIES

Every believer has a role to play—this is called a "membership ministry" in the Body of Christ. This role takes place both at church and in the community. This is the "work of the ministry" referred to in Ephesians 4:12.

Prophets, which are one of the five-fold ministries, are called and anointed to teach and activate Saints into the membership ministry of prophecy. In other words, it is the prophet's job to equip believers to hear and share the voice of God.

All five-fold ministers are given special ability from Christ to perfect, equip and mature the saints. A key to releasing spiritual ministry in our own lives is by having five-fold ministers who are willing to move in the Spirit and willing to train and allow others to exercise their spiritual senses.

The prophet's divine enablements are more than gifts of the Holy Spirit; they are the very abilities and graces of Christ. The prophet is given the special ability to know God's gifts and callings in a person's life. His words have the Christ-gifted, creative ability to impart, birth and activate that ministry into the member.

EACH BELIEVER IS MADE AN ABLE MINISTER OF THE SPIRIT

As part of our role, God enables every believer to minister by His Spirit. This is how He builds His Kingdom:

> *"Not that we are sufficient of ourselves to think of anything as being from ourselves, but our sufficiency is from God, who also made us sufficient as ministers of the new covenant, not of the letter but of the Spirit; for the letter kills, but the Spirit gives life." (2 Corinthians 3:5-6)*

God gives believers diverse graces, anointing, enablements and gifts. Through these, every member of the Body of Christ is called to move, flow, and minister in the supernatural gifts of the Holy Spirit. As Paul said in 1 Corinthians 2:4-5:

> *"And my speech and my preaching were not with persuasive words of human wisdom, but in demonstration of the Spirit and of power, that your faith should not be in the wisdom of men but in the power of God."*

As we obey 1 Peter 4:10-11, and minister in these various gifts, we will fulfill Ephesians 4:16:

"From whom the whole body, joined and knit together by what every joint supplies, according to the effective working by which every part does its share, causes growth of the body for the edifying of itself in love."

It is when "organized and knitted" members of the Body come together, each in their "effectual working," that a joining flow is formed. That is where the needs of the Body are met in love.

8

Five Methods of Prophesying

"For you can all prophesy one by one, that
all may learn, and all may be encouraged."
1 Corinthians 14:31

In our final chapter we will explore and explain the five different methods of prophetic function: the office of the prophet, prophetic preaching, prophetic presbytery, the Holy Spirit gifting of prophecy, and the spirit of prophecy. It is important to keep in mind that these expressions of prophetic ministry and function are subordinate to Scripture and must submit to Scripture in their function.

THE OFFICE OF THE PROPHET

THE OFFICE OF THE PROPHET IS A HEADSHIP MINISTRY

The office of the prophet is a leadership role God has given to the Body of Christ. It is part of the leadership of Jesus himself:

> *Therefore He says: "When He ascended on high, he led captivity captive, and gave gifts to men […] and He Himself gave some to be apostles, some prophets, some evangelists, and some pastors and teachers."'(Ephesians 4:8,11)*

When Jesus established the Church under all his authority and headship, he did not leave the church without a leadership structure in his absence:

> *"And God has appointed these in the church: first apostles, second prophets, third teachers…" (1 Corinthians 12:28)*

Jesus was the full manifestation of all five of the headship ministry callings. After His ascension, He took of His mantle and divided it among men as five-fold offices for the purpose of equipping the saints. These ministries are not an extension of Body ministry, but an extension of the headship of Christ to His Body, the Church. However, Just as Jesus trained the disciples to be effective ministers, he trained and released the 70 everyday people to be effective ministers. We never know who these 70 were or what they did for a living, but they came from the people who followed Jesus and listened to His teaching. After being trained by him, Jesus sent them out to do the work He had trained them to do.

Five-fold leaders are to do what Jesus did, train every believer to be an effective minister out in their community. As a five-fold minister, these people are an extension of the headship of Christ to His Body.

The following are scriptural examples of Jesus demonstrating each of His headship roles:

- Jesus *the* Apostle (Hebrews 3:1)
- Jesus *the* Prophet (Acts 3:22)
- Jesus *the* Evangelist (Matthew 4:23)
- Jesus *the* Pastor (John 10:14)
- Jesus *the* Teacher (John 3:2)

The office of the prophet is not the same as the gift of prophecy which comes from the Holy Spirit. The office of the prophet is a gift extension of Jesus Christ Himself as the Prophet. Jesus has chosen and anointed headship ministers, which we call offices. New Testament prophets of today receive those attributes of Christ that endow Him with ability to perceive what is in the heart of people; they enable Him to proclaim the future counsels and purposes of God, and to know the secret things of God. The following are examples of the attributes of Christ (Ephesians 2:20; Acts 13:1).

- The apostle is given that portion of Christ's mantle that is sent to establish the government and order of God.
- The evangelist receives Christ's evangelistic anointing.
- The pastor is given Christ's Good Shepherd heart and staff.
- The teacher is given Christ's divine ability to teach.

THE OFFICE OF THE PROPHET IS A HIGHER RESPONSIBILITY THAN THE GIFT OF PROPHECY

The prophet is a governmental authority and role. The office of the prophet is authorized, enabled, and designed to function in a higher realm of ministry than the Holy Spirit gift of prophecy (which is for edification, exhortation, and comfort). The office has the same authority to minister to the Church with preaching and prophesying as the pastor does with preaching and pastoral counseling. This does not mean that anyone who feels called as a prophet has the right to override the senior pastor's position or judgments in the local church. Each has a special anointing and ability for unique ministry.

As part of the Ekklesia, a prophet may operate in business (like Joseph), government (like Daniel or David), or any area of influence within a community or a nation. It is one of the five-fold headship ministries that flow and work with all headship ministries.

All five-fold ministers are given special ability from Christ to perfect, equip and mature the saints. This office functions in all the ministries of the Old and New Testaments, and stand in the role of Christ, *the* Prophet. Therefore, a prophet's prophecies flow in the areas of guidance, instruction, rebuke, judgment and revelation—however Christ chooses to speak for the purifying and perfection of His Church.

The prophet is given the special ability to know God's gifts and callings in a person's life and to activate saints into their membership ministry. The prophet's perception in this area is higher and more anointed than those with the gift of prophecy—they are the very abilities and graces of Christ. When the prophet lays hands on and prophesies gifts and callings to a person, his or her words have the Christ-gifted creative ability to impart, birth and activate that ministry into the member. If the person receiving the prophetic word does not receive it in faith, there will still be a birthing—but it will be stillborn. (Read page 27, *Prophets and Personal Prophecy*.)

SOME AREAS THE PROPHET MAY FUNCTION

While any believer can minister prophetically, the prophet does so with greater responsibility and authority. This is because the purpose of the prophet is different; the goal is to build the church and provide the plumb line for the voice of God being released in the Earth. Here are some of the functions of ministry from a prophet:

- Provide direction (1 Kings 22:7; 2 Kings 5:10).
- Offer correction through the permission of the pastor (Ezekiel 3:18).
- Pronounce divine decrees of God's judgments or blessings, as evident in major portions of Old Testament prophets.
- Move in revelation knowledge (Isaiah 44:28-45:3 was prophesied in 750 BC but was fulfilled in 650 BC—150 years later, as described in Daniel 10.)
- Lay foundations in the Church, especially the apostle/prophet, to teach, train, activate, speak into leadership (Ephesians 2:20).
- Impart spiritual gifts (1 Timothy 4:14).
- Anoint ministries. The prophets anointed the three ministries of the Old Testament: The first king (Saul) was anointed by the prophet Samuel (1 Samuel 10:1); The first High Priest (Aaron) was anointed by the prophet Moses

(Exodus 28:41; Psalm 133:2); Prophets are anointed by other prophets (Elijah anointed Elisha, 1 Kings 19:16).

- Partake of the secrets of God. "Surely the Lord God does nothing, unless He reveals His secret to His servants the prophets," (Amos 3:7).
- Stir up, challenge, and bring things out of dormancy to move forward by the Word of the Lord. Haggai stirred up the builders and people who then said, "We must build!"

Jesus has set five headship ministry gifts in the Church to minister the written (logos) Word and the quickened (rhema) word. The five-fold ministers should spend as much time in preparation to move in the Spirit as they do in preparing to deliver a sound scriptural teaching. A great key to releasing spiritual ministry is to have five-fold ministers who are willing to move in the Spirit and are also willing to train and allow others to exercise their spiritual senses.

PROPHETIC PREACHING

Prophesying and preaching are not the same; however, a preacher may include prophesy in their message, or may even deliver a prophetic message. Normally, preaching is speaking biblical truths that have been researched, studied, and arranged for presentation. These truths are eternal, and the Holy Spirit will bring illumination to the hearer and the speaker when Scriptures are ministered. Preaching proclaims the logos with the Holy Spirit's ability to bring greater understanding. Prophecy, on the other hand, gives a rhema. Prophecy is normally by divine inspiration and revelation knowledge—it is spontaneous.

PROPHETIC PREACHING IS ON A DIFFERENT LEVEL

Prophetic preaching is on a different level than preaching and has a number of different qualities. Preaching is very appropriate and comprises the majority of messages delivered by ministers. Training on preparation of sermons (homiletics) and how to deliver them (pulpit speech) is customary. Preachers may have prepared notes and have general thoughts in mind, but they allow God to fill them in as they minister. Although such preaching is anointed and led by the Holy Spirit, it is not necessarily prophetic preaching. The minister who is sensitive to the Holy Spirit should be preaching messages at God's direction. A prophetic message has its place—though it does not seem to constitute the majority of the messages God has a minister deliver.

Prophetic preaching is characterized by certain attributes. First, it must be biblical truth. Just as with prophecy, the prophetic message is subordinate to the Word of God (which is the standard by which we judge). Second, it is by the unction of the Holy Spirit that the speaker's words and illustrations are exactly what God wants to say. The preacher is directed to share certain truths, but he is also directed to say them in a certain way—by using divinely directed illustrations. These illustrations impact the hearers uniquely because they are chosen specifically for them. Third, there is impact and accuracy in the word; it is meant for the people present at the time. Although the truths are biblical and would be of benefit to anyone who hears them, they are specifically directed to those present and represent a significant relevance to the hearers. Therefore, prophetic instructions and admonitions given during the prophetic preaching are to be treated as prophecy—they may not apply to the Body of Christ at large. Any five-fold minister can engage and function in prophetic preaching at the direction of the Lord; it is not restricted to just prophets.

PROPHETIC PRESBYTERY

Prophetic presbytery is a method for prophetic ministry by a team of men and women of God who prophesy and meet the qualifications of presbyter. This does not eliminate the need for the individual office of the prophet or a proven minister who ministers in the prophetic realm.

FUNCTIONS OF THE PROPHETIC PRESBYTERY

A prophetic presbytery is a gathering of proven ministers or prophets for a variety of purposeful ministry. One purpose is the prophetic revelation and confirmation of those called to leadership ministry in the Church (Acts 13:1-3). This allows for a believer to embrace a leadership call on his or her life, and for the leaders around to be certain as well. Another purpose is the ordination to the five-fold ministry (Titus 1:5). It is in this type of ordination that authority and gifts are imparted to the ministry through the laying on of hands. Another purpose is the confirmation and activation of membership ministries in the Body of Christ.

In Acts 6:3, the leaders perceived Stephen's gifting—in verse 6, hands were laid upon him for activation into that ministry. Prophetic presbytery teams deposit something that causes activation. They are a building block to progress believers in Christian maturity. Progression in Christian ministry is pictured in Acts 14:21-23 with a presbytery in action. The presbytery in that instance served both to benefit the saints (v. 22) and ordain to ministry. It is a strategic time and demands stewardship of both the whole, and the individual.

THE GIFT OF PROPHECY

THIS IS A GIFT, NOT AN OFFICE

Prophecy is an extension of the ministry of the Holy Spirit. It is not the same as the office of prophet, which is an extension of the ministry of Christ. It is a Body ministry function that the whole body of Christ can expect to release, while the office is a headship function. Prophecy is one of the nine manifestations of the Holy Spirit for edification, exhortation, and comfort of God's people (1 Corinthians 12, 14:3). To the unbeliever, prophecy can produce deep conviction:

> *"But if all prophesy, and an unbeliever or an uninformed person comes in, he is convinced by all, he is convicted by all. And thus the secrets of his heart are revealed; and so, falling down on his face, he will worship God and report that God is truly among you." (1 Corinthians 14:24-25)*

It is a gift. As a gift, prophecy fits these criteria:
- It is received by grace and faith (Romans 12:6; Galatians 3:5)
- It is received the same as salvation (Ephesians

2:8; Romans 14:23)
- It is not based on Christian maturity (Acts 10:45)
- It is not based on knowledge of correct doctrine (Acts 19:1 -6)
- It cannot be earned (1 Corinthians 4:7)
- It cannot be purchased (Acts 8:18)

Like all nine of the gifts of the Holy Spirit, gift of prophecy is given to any who believe, without prejudice or repentance.

The Importance of the Gift of Prophecy

Prophecy is the most edifying gift for the whole congregation (1 Corinthians 14:5). The other eight gifts are focused "rifle" gifts, normally blessing one or a few specific people. Prophecy is a "shotgun" gift that can bless hundreds of people at once. This is one reason why Paul told the saints in Corinth to: "Pursue love, and desire spiritual gifts, but especially that you may prophesy […] Therefore, brethren, desire earnestly to prophesy, and do not forbid to speak with tongues (1 Corinthians 14:1,39). He told the Thessalonians to "despise not prophesying" (1 Thessalonians 5:20). To the church at Rome he wrote: "Having then gifts differing according to the grace that is given to us, let us use them: if prophecy, let us prophesy in proportion to our faith." (Romans 12:6)

Prophesying was evidently a common event in all the churches Paul established. God puts much emphasis and validation on prophecy, for it is a powerful gift that has eternal consequences. Healing only lasts a lifetime; a word from God can change your soul forever!

> *"And it shall come to pass in the last days, says God, that I will pour out of My Spirit on all flesh; your sons and your daughters shall prophesy, your young men shall see visions, your old men shall dream dreams." (Acts 2:17)*

THE SPIRIT OF PROPHECY

The spirit of prophecy is the testimony of Jesus: "Worship God: for the testimony of Jesus is the spirit of prophecy" (Revelation 19:10). This is not a gift nor an office, but rather an anointing from Christ and arises within the believer and takes place on occasions of special anointing. The Spirit of prophecy implies that the presence of Jesus is manifesting in a way to cause believers to easily testify of Him by prophesying.

WHEN TO EXPECT THE SPIRIT OF PROPHECY

Those who are not prophets or do not have the gift of prophecy activated in them will normally not prophesy; but when the spirit of prophecy is present, they may do so, sometimes even to their own surprise. It is a special provision by the Spirit and frequently happens under one of three conditions: a strong presence of God, a gathering of prophets, or a challenge from a prophetic minister.

1. When a mighty prophetic presence of the Lord permeates the atmosphere, it can make it easier to prophesy than to keep silent. A feeling starts percolating and the heart starts beating; a thought keeps coming to you and you are compelled to speak (Read Job 32:18- 20). It is sovereign; it is not limited to two or three (as are the prophets) but as all in the service yield to the Holy Spirit.

2. When people come unto a company of prophets or under the mantle of a senior anointed prophet, the spirit of prophecy is stirred. This happened to Saul when he came into the company of prophets and prophesied.

3. When people are challenged by a minister to let God arise and testify through them by the spirit of prophecy. It is during these times that any saint can enter in and exercise faith to prophesy: "Let us prophesy in proportion to our faith" (Romans 12:6); "For you can all prophesy one by one, that all may learn and all may be encouraged" (1 Corinthians 14:31).

SCRIPTURAL EXAMPLES OF THE SPIRIT OF PROPHECY

Here are further scriptural examples of the spirit of prophecy in operation:

- God took the prophetic spirit of Moses and placed it on the seventy elders and they began to prophesy (Numbers 11:24-30).
- Saul met a company of prophets, and the spirit of prophecy came upon him so that he began to prophesy (1 Samuel 10:10).
- The Spirit of the Lord came upon Saul's messengers and they prophesied (1 Samuel 19:20-24).
- Jahaziel prophesied to Jehoshaphat (2 Chronicles 20:12-17).
- Zechariah prophesied repentance (2 Chronicles 24:20).

RELATIONSHIP IS THE KEY

The key to moving in prophecy is relationship. Those who desire to learn how to prophesy need to relate to the Holy Spirit, relate to prophetic ministers, and find a prophet or company of prophets to train and release their faith with. Building relationships with people who have a prophetic gift, are prophets, or function in the spirit of prophecy, will increase the believer's faith and activation in hearing God. But most of all, a deeper and constant communion with the Lord brings about confidence in hearing His voice: "My sheep listen to my voice; I know them, and they follow me" (John 10:27).

Endnotes

1   Genesis 1:3, 6, 9, 11, 14, 15, 20, 24

2   Genesis 2:16, 3:8, 10, 13, 17

3   Genesis 3:14

4   Genesis 4:6, 7, 9-12, 15.

5   Genesis 5:24

6   Genesis 6:13, 7:1, 8:15, 9:1, 17

7   Genesis 21:1, 4, 7, 13:14; 15:1-9; 17:13, 9, 15, 18, 19, 22, 18:1, 13, 17, 20; 20:3-7; 21:12, 17; 22:1, 2, 15

8   Genesis 16:7-13

9   Genesis 25:23; 26:2,24

10   Genesis 28:13, 31:3, 11; 35:1, 10, 11, 15

11   Genesis 31:24, 29

12   Genesis 37:5

13   Genesis 46:2

14   Genesis 41:28

15   Revelation 5:10; 20:6; 22:5; 2 Timothy 2:12

16   John 14:26; 16:13; 1 John 2:20-21, 27

17   Luke 22:31-34, 2 Samuel 12:7-13, Matthew 9:2-6, Acts 9:11-12, 17

18   Mark 5:8- 9, Acts 16:16-18

19   1 Corinthians 14:29; 1 Thessalonians 5:20-21

20   2 Corinthians 5:7 "for we walk by faith, not by sight'; Mark 5:34; 10:52; Luke 7:9,50; 8:48; Romans 3:28; 10:17; 11; Galatians 3:24; Hebrews 10:38; 11:1,3-9,11,13,17,20-24,27-33,39; 1 John 5:5.

21   Psalms 22:3; 27:14; 63:5; 92:1; 107:8,9.

Made in the USA
Columbia, SC
09 November 2024